First Knits

First Knits

Luise Roberts and Kate Haxell

Martingale
& COMPANY

With love and thanks to Margaret Roberts and Sybil Hill
who patiently taught us to knit.

Copyright © Collins & Brown Limited 2005
Text copyright © Luise Roberts and Kate Haxell 2005
Illustrations copyright © Collins & Brown Limited 2005
Photographs copyright © Collins & Brown Limited 2005

The rights of Luise Roberts and Kate Haxell to be identified as the authors of this work has
been asserted by them in accordance with the Copyright, Designs and Patents Act, 1988.

Martingale & Company
20205 144th Ave. NE
Woodinville, WA 98072-8478 USA
www.martingale-pub.com
10 09 08 07   6 5

Martingale
& C O M P A N Y

Library of Congress Cataloging-in-Publication Data is available.
ISBN: 978-1-56477-560-3

Edited and designed by Collins & Brown Limited

Mission Statement
Dedicated to providing quality products and service to inspire creativity.

EDITOR: Kate Haxell
DESIGNER: Luise Roberts
PHOTOGRAPHER: Matthew Dickens
PATTERN CHECKER: Marilyn Wilson

Reproduction by Classic Scan Pte Ltd, Singapore
Printed in China by SNP Leefung Printers Limited

Contents

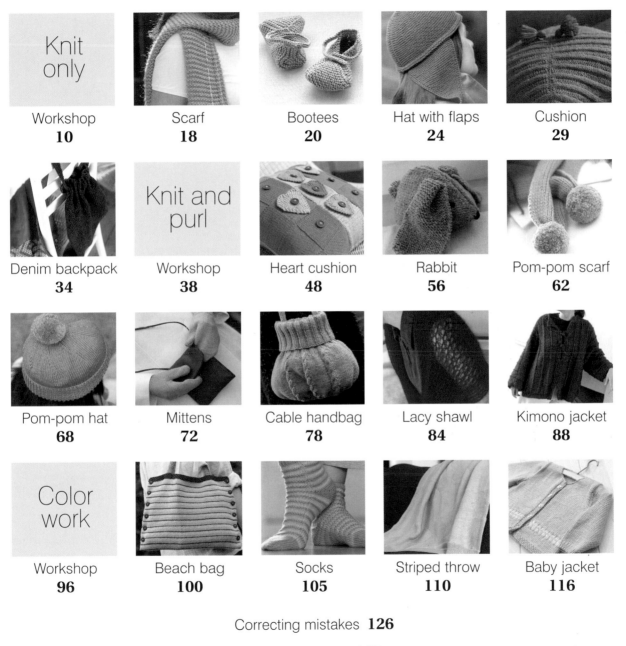

How to use this book

The fact that you have picked up this book means that you have an idea of the potiential joys of knitting, but like all new subjects there are a few things that may seem strange to begin with. This book will introduce you step-by-step to the language and techniques so you will find practical help at every step of knitting and all that will be left to you to do is practice and enjoy yourself.

This book is divided into three chapters: Knit Only, Knit and Purl, and Color Work. Each chapter starts with a workshop that will introduce the techniques used in that chapter, and each chapter builds on the skills learned in the last. All of the projects in this book are written in simple language and are designed to introduce just a few new techniques at a time, building up confidence steadily and surely. It might be a good idea to start with either the Scarf on pages 18–19 or the Bootees on pages 20–23 because they will you a good grounding in knit stitch and would make perfect gifts if you choose not to keep them yourself. However, it is not necessary to knit every project in the book because nothing is over-complicated or difficult, and the step-by-step photographs and cross referencing to the workshops and flaps ensure that the helping hand of an experienced knitter is always with you. This is not a college course or an exam you have to get high grades in. Don't expect perfection the first time, and remember to enjoy the process of knitting.

This practical help will also be available when things go wrong. The section on correcting mistakes

Step One

Read the Getting Started pages and find a pair of old needles and an odd scrap of yarn. However, it isn't easy to knit a fine yarn with very large needles, and very chunky yarn and large needles can also be very unwieldy, especially when you are unfamiliar with the techniques. If possible, check a ball band for suggested needle sizes, but for the first experiment you can make do. Turn to the first workshop.

on pages 126–127 is well worth a read before you start so you will know what to do if things do go wrong.

Finally, when starting any new hobby it is always tempting to limit expenditure until you discover if this is the pastime for you. However, this can be a mistake with knitting. The yarns in this book have been selected because they are of the highest quality, which means they will produce the best results. Good yarn is also easier to use, less likely to split and has fewer knots and unevenness along its length. Look at the yarn information on pages 127–128, search out the bargain basements, ask knitting friends if they have any yarn they can spare and talk to the staff in the yarn stores. Knitters are often evangelistic about their skill and eager to help. Having said that you should buy quality yarn, many of the projects in this book only use two or three balls, so they aren't expensive to complete.

Workshop

WORKSHOP • KNIT ONLY

Before starting any of the projects in this chapter, practice the techniques with the following swatches; the finished projects will be far more successful. This first workshop introduces casting on, binding (casting) off and the basic knit stitch, which will be found in every knitting project in this book.

1 Slip knot
The first stitch in all knitting is the slip knot.

1 Loop the yarn twice around your fingers with the second loop lying behind the first one. Use the tip of a knitting needle to draw the second loop through the first one.

2 Pull the the ends of the yarn to tighten the loop around the needle.

You will need

Any durable yarn can be used. Check the manufacturer's band for information on the suggested needle sizes and if a range is suggested, choose the middle size.
The yarn and needles used for the practice swatches in this book are:

Rowan All Seasons Cotton 1⅔oz (50g)

1 pair US 7 (4.5mm) needles

Gauge (tension)
The gauge (tension) does not matter too much at this stage; just concentrate on achieving a

Step Two

Each chapter starts with a workshop with step-by-step diagrams showing the numbered techniques that will be introduced in the chapter. These are followed by practice swatches so you can try out the techniques before starting a project. This is not a wasted effort; if the same yarn and needles are used for each swatch, they can be pieced together to make a cushion, bag or small throw. Repeat each swatch until you are confident with the result.

Scarf

SCARF • KNIT ONLY

This is the ideal project for a knitting novice. It is simple to work, "grows" quickly and produces a luxurious result. One size fits all, so no gauge (tension) swatch is needed.

Size
9½ × 70 in. (24 × 180 cm)

You will need
Four 3½oz (100g) balls of Rowan Polar in fawn

US 11 (8mm) needles
Tapestry needle
Two 80 in. (200 cm) lengths of ⅛-in. (4-mm) wide silk ribbon, 1 in mauve and 1 in pink

Making the scarf

Make a **slip knot 1** 20 in. (50 cm) from the end of the yarn and, using the **thumb cast-on method 2**, cast on 30 sts.

ROW 1: **Slip 1 knitwise (sl1 lwise) 3**. **knit (k) 4** to end of row.

Rep row 1 until you are nearing the end of the first ball of yarn.

To estimate how many rows can be knitted with the remaining yarn, lay the work flat on a surface. Lay the yarn backwards and forwards across the row of stitches, as shown. To knit one row, you need approximately enough yarn to go four times across the width of the stitches. If you don't have at least this much left, attach a new ball of yarn.

To attach another ball of yarn 5, make a single knot in the new yarn, about 4 in. (10 cm) from the end. Draw the tail end of the old yarn through the knot and pull the knot tight at the base of the last stitch on the previous row. Continue (cont) to knit as before.

Knit until all four balls of yarn have been used and you have enough left for one row.

Bind (cast) off 6.

Cut the yarn leaving a tail approximately 4 in. (10 cm) long. Carefully take the stitch off the needle and thread the cut end of the yarn through it. Pull gently on the cut end to close up the stitch.

Finishing

Weave in ends 7 of the yarn along the edges where the new balls were joined, and on the cast-on and bound (cast) off edges.

Tie a knot in one end of the mauve length of silk ribbon. Trim the end close to the knot. Thread the other end through the tapestry needle and take the needle through the loop of the third stitch along the cast-on edge. Then push the needle through the ribbon, just above the knot. Pull the ribbon up so that the end is wrapped tightly around the stitch.

Work running stitch up the edge of the scarf. Take the needle over one ridge (two rows), then under a loop on the next ridge. Make sure that you go under the same stitch in from the edge each time to keep the running stitch straight. If the ribbon twists, pull it loose again and untwist it before moving on to the next stitch.
Keep the knitting flat and do not pull the running stitches too tight or the edge of the knitting will become distorted.
At the other end of the scarf, secure the ribbon by knotting it tightly around a stitch on the bound (cast) off edge.
Rep the process with the second length of ribbon 6 stitches farther in from the edge

STEP-BY-STEP IMAGES
Show what you should have on your needles.

18   The numbers in the squares refer to instructions in the Workshop sections   19

EQUIPMENT AND YARN INFORMATION
Make sure you have everything you need before you start.

TECHNIQUES
The first time a technique appears in a pattern it is written out in full and cross-referred to the workshops and extended flaps by a number. The abbreviated initials for the technique are also given in brackets.

Step Three

Select at least two patterns from each chapter before going on to the next. Read through the pattern to get a general idea of how it is shaped, but if there is a bit you are not quite sure about, don't despair, it will all become clear when you come to knit it. Use the extended flaps for a quick reminder of the techniques already practiced in the workshops and the abbreviations used. And study the photographs—they are there to help.

Getting started

One of the joys of knitting is its simplicity. It is a skill that has been honed by generations of fingers, and requires only two long sticks, the yarn of your choice and one basic stitch to begin. There is no set way of holding your yarn or needles, although there are some that are more popular than others and are suggested here to get you started. Knitting is about the process of creating a unique fabric and the peace that is found as the industrious rhythm of fingers allows the mind to wander.

KNITTING NEEDLES
The type used in this book are made of bamboo and are ideal for beginners because they are light and the stitches are less likely to slide off them than with metal needles. Check the needles carefully before buying to make sure there is no pitting in the surface and that the points are round and smooth. A longer point is useful on thinner sizes.

CABLE NEEDLE
This is used for holding stitches to one side while others are worked within a repeat. Look for a cable needle with a bend in it because it holds the stitches more securely.

STITCH HOLDER
This is used to hold a large number of stitches to one side while rows of other stitches are worked.

Equipment

The pattern will tell you at the start what equipment is required to knit the project. The most important purchase is that of the knitting needles. These come in a range of diameters, which are either described in metric millimeters or by one of two sizing systems. Check the pattern carefully and if you are unsure, ask in the store before purchase. However, the pattern will give a suggested size only to achieve the correct number of stitches and rows in a given distance. If it is important that the knitted project exactly matches the size given in the pattern, for instance in the case of a garment, then purchase at the same time one needle size up and one down from that suggested. You will love knitting, and these needles will be used for another project one day.

RULER
A plastic or metal ruler is less likely to become distorted and is useful to check the gauge (tension). The one shown above is a special gauge with a sliding pointer.

TAPE MEASURE
Useful for greater distances and checking project measurements.

SNIPPERS
These are spring-loaded so that they are always ready to use and they spring back to the open position each time. However, any small, sharp-pointed scissors can be used.

SEWING NEEDLE
These should be blunt and round-pointed with a large eye. A sharp-pointed needle is more likely to split the yarn.

Holding the yarn

The working yarn is held under tension in order to make it easier to control and regulate the stitch size and tension. There are various methods of doing this, but these are two of the most common. Try them both and choose the one you are most comfortable with.

Pass the yarn under the little finger and middle finger to rest over the index finger. This method gives a slightly looser tension.

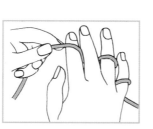

Loop the yarn around the little finger and then under the middle finger to rest over the index finger. This method gives a slightly tighter tension.

You may find that you do not use one method exclusively, but change depending on the pattern being knitted or the yarn used. Some yarns are more slippery and some patterns, such as rib, benefit from a tighter tension.

If you are working the yarn in your left hand both methods can be used. In the left hand method the index finger is held upwards (see right), holding the yarn in tension from the needle so that the right needle can draw it through the stitch loop.

Holding the needles

There is no right way and no wrong way to hold knitting needles. The various methods fall into two categories—those that hold the yarn being worked in the right hand and those that hold it in the left. Holding the yarn in the left hand is often described as the "Continental method" and has the benefit of fewer hand and finger movements. Holding the yarn in the right hand is more common in the United States and the United Kingdom and, because it often uses an individual's stronger hand, is easier to learn.

Initially knitting will seem awkward whichever hand you use. Try both ways, but if you do know an experienced knitter, there are advantages to using the same hand used by them. They can guide you as you extend your knitting repertoire, as there are subtly different ways in how a left hander and right hander perform the same technique. The step-by-step photography and illustrations in this book have been designed to accommodate both methods.

Holding the yarn in the right hand

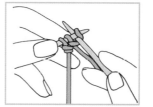 

The left needle is held from above, almost hanging from the left hand.

Hold the needle in the right hand as if you are holding a pencil.

Holding the yarn in the left hand

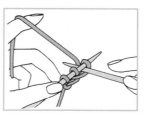

The left needle is held by the thumb and middle finger with the yarn held aloft by the index finger.

Knit only

Workshop

Before starting any of the projects in this chapter, practice the techniques with the following swatches; the finished projects will be far more successful. This first workshop introduces casting on, binding (casting) off and the basic knit stitch, which will be found in every knitting project in this book.

You will need
Any durable yarn can be used. Check the manufacturer's band for information on the suggested needle sizes and if a range is suggested, choose the middle size.
The yarn and needles used for the practice swatches in this book are:

Rowan All Seasons Cotton 1¾oz (50g)

1 pair US 7 (4.5mm) needles

Gauge (tension)
The gauge (tension) does not matter too much at this stage; just concentrate on achieving a comfortable flow that will keep the stitches even.

The numbers in the squares refer to instructions in the Workshop sections.

1 Slip knot
The first stitch in all knitting is the slip knot.

1 Loop the yarn twice around your fingers with the second loop lying behind the first one. Use the tip of a knitting needle to draw the second loop through the first one.

2 Pull the the ends of the yarn to tighten the loop around the needle.

2 Thumb cast-on method

This cast-on is particularly elastic and looks good with the knit stitch.

1 Make a slip knot 12 in. (30 cm) from the end of the yarn. Hold the needle with the knot in the right hand. ✳ Wind the loose end of the yarn around the left thumb, from front to back. Wind the ball end of the yarn around the right index finger. Put the tip of the needle under the loop of yarn around the thumb, as shown.

Note: the position of the slip knot will vary depending on the number of stitches to be cast on: 12 in. (30 cm) is enough for 15 sts.

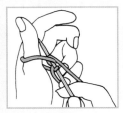

2 With the right index finger, take the ball end of the yarn over the tip of the needle. Drop the yarn off the finger.

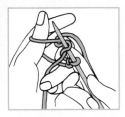

3 Pull the loop made by the ball end of the yarn through the loop around the thumb, slipping the loop off the thumb as you do so. Gently pull the loose end to close the stitch.✳

4 Repeat from ✳ to ✳ until the number of stitches stated in the pattern, including the slip knot, are on the needle.

To practice this stitch

Cast on 15 sts using the thumb cast-on method.

3 Knit stitch (k)

This is one of the two basic stitches used in knitting.

1 Hold the needle with the cast-on stitches in the left hand and an empty needle in the right hand. Insert the right-hand needle through the first stitch from left to right.

2 Take the yarn around the tip of the right-hand needle, going underneath and then across the top of the needle.

3 Use the tip of the needle to pull the loop of yarn through the stitch on the left-hand needle. This makes a new stitch on the right-hand needle.

4 As you pull the yarn through, allow the original stitch to slip off the left-hand needle, keeping the new stitch on the right-hand needle.

5 Repeat these four steps for each stitch on the left-hand needle. This is one row. Now put the right needle in the left hand and repeat the procedure with the new stitches. A pattern of repeated rows of knit stitch is known as garter stitch.

To practice this stitch

Cast on 15 sts using the thumb cast-on method. For this swatch continue until 27 rows have been completed.

4 Counting rows and stitches

In order to determine the gauge (tension) it is necessary to count the rows and stitches. In the swatch below, the first two rows after the cast-on row have been knitted in a contrasting color. From this it is possible to see that one ridge equals two rows. When counting rows for a pattern, you do not count the cast-on row, but you do count the row of stitches that is on the needle.

To count the number of stitches either make a note while the stitches are still on the needle or study the image to the right, which shows one stitch knitted in a contrasting color.

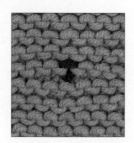

5 Attaching another ball of yarn

Unless a project is very small, more than one ball of yarn will be required. A new ball is best attached at the end of a row. As a rough guide, enough yarn to span about four times the width of a row is required in order to complete the row, though this does vary slightly from pattern to pattern. If you don't have at least this much, then attach a new ball before beginning the next row.

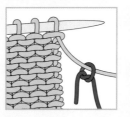

Make a single knot in the new yarn. Draw the tail end of the old yarn through the knot and pull the knot tight at the base of the last stitch on the previous row. Weave in the ends when the project has been completed.

6 Weaving in ends

Thread the needle with the end of the yarn. Take the needle under the loops of four or five stitches adjacent to the point where the end appears. Pull the yarn through. Stretch the knitting a little to ensure that the woven-in end is not too tight. Skip the stitch the needle came out of and repeat the process in the other direction, going back under the same stitches. Stretch the knitting a little, as before; then cut the end off close to the work.

The numbers in the squares refer to instructions in the Workshop sections.

7 Bind (cast) off garter stitch

This is a method of permanently securing the loops of the knitting. To bind or cast off means the same thing. In America knitters tend to be more familiar with the term "bind off" and in Britain knitters tend to say "cast off".

1 Knit two stitches. Insert the left-hand needle into the stitch farthest from the tip of the right-hand needle. Pass this stitch over the other stitch and drop it off both needles.

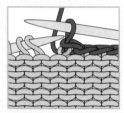

2 Knit another stitch, insert the left-hand needle into the stitch farthest from the tip of the right-hand needle, and repeat as before.

3 Repeat these steps until one stitch remains on the right-hand needle. Cut the yarn, leaving a tail about 4 in. (10 cm) long. Take the stitch off the needle, pull the end through it and gently pull the end to close up the stitch.

To practice this stitch
Bind (cast) off the swatch used to practice the knit stitch.

8 Measure the swatch

Knitting is a handicraft that varies from person to person. All knitting patterns give the gauge (tension) required. This is the number of stitches and rows over a given distance that will reproduce a finished piece to match the original created by the knitting designer.

Before starting any project it is important to check your gauge (tension). Knit a swatch a few stitches wider and a few rows longer than the gauge (tension) given. This block of knitting can then be compared to the specifications given in the knitting pattern.

Lay the swatch flat without stretching it. Lay a ruler or measuring gauge horizontally across the stitches and mark the distance specified with pins. Count the number of stitches between the pins.

Repeat the process laying the ruler vertically and count the number of rows between the pins.

If the number of stitches and rows is greater than specified in the pattern, knit the swatch again using larger needles. If it is less, try smaller needles.

If the yarn and needles specified on page 11 were used to make this practice swatch, the gauge (tension) should be 11 stitches and 16 rows to 2 in. (5 cm) of garter stitch.

9 Slip stitch knitwise (sl1 kwise)

The slip stitch is useful as a simple way to work neat edges on garter stitch, as well as a way to add an alternative texture.

Insert the right-hand needle through the stitch on the left-hand needle from front to back, with the working yarn at the back of the needles. Move the stitch off the left-hand needle and onto the right-hand needle.

10 Slip stitch purlwise (sl1 pwise)

This slip stitch can be worked on a purl or knit row, but the yarn must be in front of the work.

With the yarn at the front, slip 1 stitch purlwise by putting the needle through the stitch from right to left. Move the stitch off the left-hand needle and onto the right-hand needle. Take the yarn back between the needles if necessary.

To practice this stitch

Make a **slip knot** 🔳 12 in. (30 cm) from the end of the yarn and cast on 15 sts using the **thumb cast-on method** 🔳.

ROW 1: **Knit (k)** 🔳.

ROW 2: K1, [**slip 1 purlwise (sl1 pwise)**, k1] repeat the sequence within the brackets to the end of the row. Repeat the last 2 rows twelve times more.

(26 rows)

Bind (cast) off 🔳.

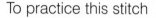

To practice this stitch

Make a **slip knot** 🔳 12 in. (30 cm) from the end of the yarn and cast on 15 sts using the **thumb cast-on method** 🔳.

Knit (k) 🔳 1 row.

With the yarn at the back of the needles **slip 1 knitwise (sl1 kwise)** at the beginning of every row for 26 rows.

(27 rows)

Bind (cast) off 🔳.

The numbers in the squares refer to instructions in the Workshop sections.

15

11 Knit two stitches together (k2tog)

Knitting two stitches together is a simple way of reducing the number of stitches on the needle and, therefore, the width of the knitted item.

Use the same action for knitting one stitch to knit two stitches together. Put the right-hand needle front to back through the second stitch from the end of the needle and then through the first stitch. Knit the two stitches as though they were one.

To practice this stitch

Make a **slip knot** 1 12 in. (30 cm) from the end of the yarn and cast on 15 sts using the **thumb cast-on method** 2.

ROWS 1–2: Knit (k) 3.

ROW 3: Knit until only 2 sts are left on the left-hand needle, **knit two stitches together (k2tog).**

(14 sts on the needle.)

ROW 4: Slip 1 purlwise (sl1 pwise) 10, knit to the end of the row.

Repeat the last 2 rows twelve times more.

(28 rows)

ROW 29: K2tog.

Cut the yarn 4 in. (10 cm) from the needle, draw the end through the last stitch and pull tight.

To create a square, knit this swatch twice and sew the diagonal edges together.

12 Yarnover (yo)

Yarnovers are a decorative way of increasing the number of stitches across a row. When used in conjunction with k2tog, a yarnover makes an eyelet, or hole.

Wrap the yarn around the right-hand needle counterclockwise, finishing in the position ready to work the next stitch.

To practice this stitch

Make a **slip knot** 1 12 in. (30 cm) from the end of the yarn and cast on 15 sts using the **thumb cast-on method** 2.

ROWS 1–4: Knit (k) 3.

PATTERN ROW 5: K2, [**knit two stitches together (k2tog)** 11, **yarnover (yo)**] repeat the sequence within the brackets four times more, k3.

PATTERN ROWS 6–8: Knit to end.

Rep the last 4 rows, four times more.

Knit 2 rows.

(26 rows)

Bind (cast) off 7.

13 Blocking and pressing

Once the pieces of a project are knitted they need to be blocked and pressed before they are sewn together. This will help to ensure that the pieces are the correct sizes and that they look their best.

To block a piece, lay it right side (RS) down on a clean padded surface. An ironing board with a towel fastened over it will work, but the best option is a specially made blocking board. This is a piece of wood with a towel folded up on it and covered with cotton fabric. The fabric should be stretched tightly and stapled to the wood on the back. Using gingham fabric is a good idea as the pattern of squares is very helpful when pinning out straight edges.

Pin the piece of knitting to the surface, putting in a pin every 1 in. (2 cm) and angling them through the very edge of the knitting into the padding.

Ensure that the lines of stitches and rows are straight and measure each piece to check that it is the correct size. If necessary, re-pin the pieces, easing in or stretching them slightly. The outline of each piece should be smooth between the pins.

The pinned-out sections of knitting are pressed to give a smooth finish and to help them hold their shape. If there are no specific instructions for pressing the yarn on the ball band, use the following as a general guide. **Natural fibers (wool, cotton, linen, etc.):** using a warm iron and damp cloth, steam the knitting thoroughly but do not allow the iron to drag on the fabric. **Synthetic fibers:** do not press 100% synthetic yarn. **Mixed fibers:** use a cool iron and a dry cloth.

After sewing up the seams, press them on the wrong side (WS) using the same method, though they do not have to be pinned.

14 Flat stitch

Unlike the other stitches in this section, this is not a knitted stitch but a seam stitch that is made using a needle and thread. Many projects have more than one piece of knitting that need to be sewn together. Flat stitch, as its name suggests, produces a flat seam that is flexible as well as strong.

Pin the two pieces wrong-sides together, matching the edges and corners. Thread a tapestry needle with a length of yarn and whipstitch the pieces together through the knots created at the end of each row, matching row to row.

To practice this stitch
Sew the five swatches from the previous pages together.

The numbers in the squares refer to instructions in the Workshop sections.

17

Scarf

This is the ideal project for a knitting novice. It is simple to work, "grows" quickly and produces a luxurious result. One size fits all, so no gauge (tension) swatch is needed.

Size

9¾ × 70 in. (24 × 180 cm)

You will need

Four 3½oz (100g) balls of Rowan Polar in fawn

US 11 (8mm) needles
Tapestry needle
Two 80 in. (200 cm) lengths of ³⁄₁₆-in. (4-mm) wide silk
  ribbon, 1 in mauve and 1 in pink

Making the scarf

Make a **slip knot** **1** 20 in. (50 cm) from the end of the yarn and, using the **thumb cast-on method** **2**, cast on 30 sts.

ROW 1: Slip 1 knitwise (sl1 kwise) 9,   **knit (k) 3** to end of row.

Rep row 1 until you are nearing the end of the first ball of yarn.

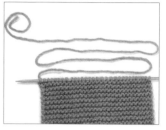

To estimate how many rows can be knitted with the remaining yarn, lay the work flat on a surface. Lay the yarn backwards and forwards across the row of stitches, as shown. To knit one row, you need approximately enough yarn to go four times across the width of the stitches. If you don't have at least this much left, attach a new ball of yarn.

To **attach another ball of yarn** 5, make a single knot in the new yarn, about 4 in. (10 cm) from the end. Draw the tail end of the old yarn through the knot and pull the knot tight at the base of the last stitch on the previous row. Continue (cont) to knit as before.

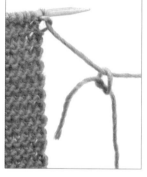

Knit until all four balls of yarn have been used and you have enough left for one row.

Bind (cast) off 7.

Cut the yarn leaving a tail approximately 4 in. (10 cm) long. Carefully take the stitch off the needle and thread the cut end of the yarn through it. Pull gently on the cut end to close up the stitch.

Finishing

Weave in ends 6 of the yarn along the edges where the new balls were joined, and on the cast-on and bound (cast) off edges.

Tie a knot in one end of the mauve length of silk ribbon. Trim the end close to the knot. Thread the other end through the tapestry needle and take

the needle through the loop of the third stitch along the cast-on edge. Then push the needle through the ribbon, just above the knot. Pull the ribbon up so that the end is wrapped tightly around the stitch.

Work running stitch up the edge of the scarf. Take the needle over one ridge (two rows), then under a loop on the next ridge. Make sure that you go under the same stitch in from the edge each time to keep the running stitch straight. If the ribbon twists, pull it loose again and untwist it before moving on to the next stitch.

Keep the knitting flat and do not pull the running stitches too tight or the edge of the knitting will become distorted.

At the other end of the scarf, secure the ribbon by knotting it tightly around a stitch on the bound (cast) off edge.

Rep the process with the second length of ribbon 6 stitches farther in from the edge.

The numbers in the squares refer to instructions in the Workshop sections.

Bootees

No shaping, no complicated stitches, and no bother. Embellish this simple bootee to make the perfect personalized baby-shower gift.

Size

This bootee is for a 6-month-old baby with a foot length of 4 in. (10 cm).

You will need

One 1¾oz (50g) ball Rowan Cotton Glace in pink

US 4 (3.5mm) needles
Tapestry needle

Gauge (tension) swatch

Make a **slip knot** **1** 16 in. (40 cm) from the end of the yarn and, using the **thumb cast-on method** **2**, cast on 26 sts.

When all the stitches have been cast on, transfer the needle to the left hand and pick up the second needle in the right hand, ready to knit.

ROW 1: **Knit (k)** **3**.

Rep row 1 until 49 rows have been worked.

Counting rows and stitches ▲. Count the number of bumps along a ridge (to find the number of stitches) and count the ridges (each ridge represents two rows).

Bind (cast) off ▼.

Measure the swatch ▣.

There should be 26 stitches and 50 rows to 4 in. (10 cm). If the gauge (tension) is correct, proceed with the project instructions.

The numbers in the squares refer to instructions in the Workshop sections.

Making the bootees
Foot (make 2)

A square is knitted to form the sole and the sides of the bootee.

If the gauge (tension) swatch has the correct number of rows and stitches to 4 in. (10 cm) then this can be used for one foot piece.

As for the gauge (tension) swatch, make a slip knot 16 in. (40 cm) from the end of the yarn and, using the thumb cast-on method, cast on 26 sts.

ROW 1: Knit.
This and all odd number rows are a right-side (RS) row.
Rep row 1 until the work measures 4 in. (10 cm) from the cast-on edge.

Bind (cast) off.

Toe (make 2)

This square is approximately a quarter of the size of the foot square.

Make a slip knot 8 in. (20 cm) from the end of the yarn and, using the thumb cast-on method, cast on 13 sts.

ROW 1: Knit.

Rep row 1 until the work measures 2 in. (5 cm) from the cast-on edge.

End with a RS row and the cast-on tail at the bottom right of the work.

There should be 23 rows or 11 knitted ridges, plus the cast-on ridge.

Bind (cast) off.

Strap (make 2)

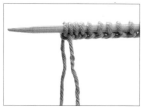

Make a slip knot 36 in. (90 cm) from the end of the yarn and, using the thumb cast-on method, cast on 60 sts.

Bind (cast) off.

Using the tapestry needle, weave in the ends.

Finishing

Block and press ⓐ all the pieces gently, taking particular care to press the edges.

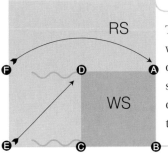

Cast-on edges

Thread the tapestry needle with a 12 in. (30 cm) length of yarn. Position the two squares on top of each other, RS facing and with the cast-on edges together.

Finish by sewing through the first corner stitch Ⓐ, as shown.

Sew the seams using **flat stitch** ⓐ. Insert the needle through the first bound (cast) off stitch on one side of the toe piece and the corresponding row end on the foot piece Ⓐ. Sew down to cast-on edge.

Turn the corner Ⓑ and cont flat stitching along the cast-on edges to Ⓒ. This time, insert the needle through the outer loops of the stitches.

Align the other cast-on corner of the foot Ⓔ with the free corner of the toe piece Ⓓ. Flat stitch from Ⓒ to corner Ⓔ Ⓓ.

Bring the edge of the foot piece that has not been stitched Ⓕ against the fourth side of the toe piece to align with Ⓐ and flat stitch this seam.

To form the heel, fold the bound (cast) off edges of the foot piece in half; then push the center of the fold halfway up the fold itself, as shown. Flat stitch the seam. Cut the tails from the cast-on and bound (cast) off rows short.

Fold the strip in half and align the fold with the heel seam. Attach the strap around the heel using flat stitch. **Weave in ends** ⓖ.

VARIATIONS
These bootees can be personalized by using two colors of yarn—one color for the toes and one for the foot. Trimmings such as ribbon or fabric flower buds can also be used. However, these must be secured firmly.

The numbers in the squares refer to instructions in the workshop sections.

Hat with flaps

This basic hat is quick and easy to knit, and it can be decorated with beads and embroidery for an individual look. You can knit it without the flaps if you prefer.

Size

Measure the head around the widest part across the forehead.
Medium head size: 21 in. (53.5 cm).
Knitted hat circumference (not stretched):
    17½ in. (44.5 cm).

You will need

Three 1¾oz (50g) balls of Rowan Wool Cotton
    in olive green

US 6 (4mm) needles
Tapestry needle

Gauge (tension) swatch

Make a **slip knot** 🔳**1** 20 in. (50 cm) from the end of the yarn, and using the **thumb cast-on method** 🔳**2**, cast on 30 sts.

ROW 1: **Knit (k)** 🔳**3**.

Rep row 1 until 60 rows have been worked.

Bind (cast) off 🔳**7**.

Measure the swatch 🔳**8**.
Counting rows and stitches 🔳**4**. There should be 25 stitches and 50 rows to 4 in. (10 cm).

Making the hat with flaps
Brim

Make a slip knot 40 in. (100 cm) from the end of the yarn and, using the thumb cast-on method, cast on 112 sts.

The numbers in the squares refer to instructions in the Workshop sections.

25

ROW 1: Knit.

Rep row 1 until the work measures 6¼ in. (16 cm) from the cast-on edge. End with a wrong-side (WS) row with the cast-on tail at the bottom left.

There should be 80 rows or 40 ridges.

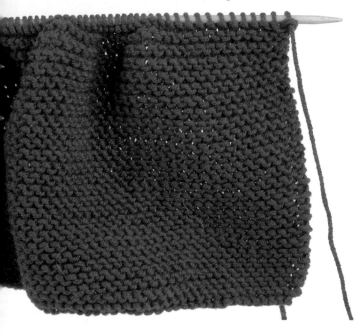

Crown

The top of the hat is shaped by reducing the number of stitches.

ROW 81: [K4, **knit two stitches together (k2tog)]** , rep the bracketed sequence until there are 4 sts on the left-hand needle, k4.

(There are now 94 sts remaining.)

ROW 82 : On this and all even-numbered rows, knit.

ROW 83: [K3, k2tog], rep to last 4 sts, k4.

(76 sts remaining)

ROW 85: [K2, k2tog], rep to end of row.

(57 sts)

ROW 87: [K1, k2tog], rep to end of row.

(38 sts)

ROW 89: K2tog, rep to end of row.

(19 sts)

ROW 91: [K1, k2tog], rep to last st, k1.

(13 sts)

ROW 93: [K1, k2tog], rep to last st, k1.

(9 sts)

ROW 95: K2tog, rep to last st, k1.

(5 sts)

Knit 4 rows.

Cut the yarn 15 in. (40 cm) from the last stitch and thread the end through a tapestry needle. Slip the stitches off the knitting needle onto the tapestry needle. Pull tight.

For the neatest edge, pull the loop of the last knitted stitch tight around the needle before drawing the yarn through.

Flaps (make 2)

Make a slip knot 20 in. (50 cm) from the end of the yarn and, using the thumb cast-on method, cast on 36 sts.

ROWS 1–8: Knit.

ROW 9: K2, k2tog, knit until there are 4 sts on the left-hand needle, k2tog, k2. *(34 sts)*

ROWS 10–12: Knit.

Rep rows 9–12 until there are 6 sts on the needle and a total of 68 rows.

ROWS 69–104: Knit.

Row 104
After 36 rows of straight knitting.

Row 68
After the decrease rows.

The numbers in the squares refer to instructions in the Workshop sections.

The stitches are decreased to form a point.

ROW 105: K2, k2tog, k2tog. *(4 sts)*

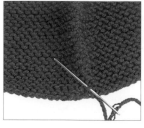

Cont until the whole seam has been stitched; then weave the end into the seam. It should be invisible on the RS.

Cont to decrease as follows (folls).

ROW 106: K1, k2tog, k1.

ROW 107: K1, k2tog.

Bind (cast) off last 2 sts.

Turn up ⅞ in. (2 cm) of the brim and pin in place. Leaving a long tail, bring the needle up at the cast-on edge. Secure the brim by stitching one row of stitch bumps on the hat to the folded-up brim edge.

Cut the yarn 4 in. (10 cm) from the last stitch and pull the stitch loose. Take the yarn through the stitch and pull it tight.

Weave in ends 6 into the fold of the brim.

Finishing

Block and press 13 all the pieces lightly, taking particular care over the edges.

Thread a tapestry needle with a 15 in. (40 cm) length of yarn. Fold the hat in half with RS facing. Starting at the center of the crown, **flat stitch 14** the back seam.

RS facing, position an ear flap so that it sits just beneath the brim and one edge aligns with the back seam. Pin and slip stitch in place as for brim. Turn the hat over and attach the other ear flap.

Cushion

The techniques used to make this cushion are easy to master and the yarn weight means that the project will knit up quickly.

Size
Cushion insert size: 16 × 16 in. (40 x 40 cm)

You will need
Three 3½oz (100g) balls of Jaeger Shetland in red

US 8 (5mm) needles
US 8 (5mm) circular needles
Pins or safety pins
Tapestry needle
Sewing needle

Two 10 in. (25 cm) zippers
Sewing thread to match the yarn
4 × 4 in. (10 x 10 cm) piece of cardboard

Gauge (tension) swatch

Make a **slip knot** **1** 20 in. (50 cm) from the end of the yarn and, using the **thumb cast-on method** **2** and US 8 (5mm) straight needles, cast on 27 sts.

ROW 1: Knit (k) **3**.

ROW 2 (WS): [K3, bring yarn forward   **slip three stitches purlwise (sl3 pwise)** **10**],   take yarn back.

Rep the stitches within the brackets three times more, knit the last 3 sts.

It is important not to pull the yarn too tight behind the slipped stitches as this will distort the final width. To help prevent this, stretch the stitches out along the needle after every repeat.

These 2 rows form the pattern (patt).

The numbers in the squares refer to instructions in the Workshop sections.

29

Cont in patt until the work measures 6 in. (15.25 cm) from the cast-on edge. End with a WS row.

Knit the next 3 rows.

NEXT ROW (WS): [K1, sl1 pwise] rep to the last st, k1.

NEXT ROW: Knit.
Rep the last 2 rows until the work measures 12 in. (30 cm) from the cast-on edge.

End with a WS row.
Bind (cast) off 7 all the stitches.

Measure the swatch 8 over the patt.
Counting rows and stitches 4.
There should be 19 stitches and 48 rows to 4 in. (10 cm). Each large slip-stitch loop counts as 2 rows.

Making the cushion

Using US 8 (5mm) circular needles in the same way as straight needles, make a slip knot 36 in. (90 cm) from the end of the yarn and, using the thumb cast-on method, cast on 111 sts.

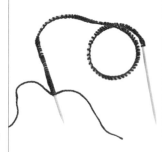

ROW 1: Knit.
ROW 2 (WS): [K3, sl3 pwise] eighteen times, k3.

The numbers in the squares refer to instructions in the Workshop sections.

Cont in patt until the work measures 10¾ in. (27.5 cm) from the cast-on edge. End with a WS row.

Knit the next 3 rows.

NEXT ROW (WS): [K1, sl1], rep to last st, k1.
NEXT ROW: Knit.
Rep the last 2 rows until the work measures 22 in. (56 cm) from the cast-on edge.

End with a WS row.
Bind (cast) off.

Finishing

Block and press ⓭ gently. Take particular care to press the edges.
Fold the corners into the center, right sides together.

Flat stitch ⓮ the two halves of the cast-on edge together. Then flat stitch the two halves of the bound (cast) off edge together.

Working from the right side, pin the closed zippers to the inside of the remaining open seams so that the pull tags are in the center and the knitting just meets over them.

The numbers in the squares refer to instructions in the Workshop sections.

Open the zippers and turn the cushion inside out. Close zippers. Thread a needle with sewing thread and, using small whip stitches, baste the zipper tapes to the WS of the cushion.

Turn the cushion right-side out and sew the zippers in place, using small back stitches close to the zipper teeth.

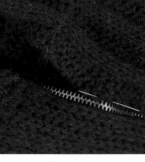

Using knitting yarn and flat stitch, close the seams between the end of the zippers and the corners. **Weave in ends 6**.

Tassels (make 2)

Wind the yarn around the cardboard twenty times.

Secure with a short length of yarn drawn under the wound yarn and tightly knotted. Take the yarn off the cardboard.

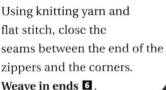

Thread a tapestry needle with yarn and wind it around the looped yarn about ¾ in. (2 cm) from the top. Use the needle to secure the yarn with small back stitches.

Cut the looped yarn. Tie a tassel to each zipper tag.

Denim backpack

This practical bag is made from a knitted rectangle and two knitted strips, which act as both straps and the bag closure. The denim yarn will fade with washing, just like jeans.

Size

When washed: 13½ × 11 in. (34 × 28 cm)

You will need

Five 1¾oz (50g) balls of Rowan Denim in blue

US 6 (4mm) and US 10 (6mm) needles
Tapestry needle
55 in. (140 cm) of 1-in. (2.5-cm) wide
    navy blue grosgrain ribbon
Sewing needle
Navy blue sewing thread

Gauge (tension) swatch

Make a **slip knot** **1** 20 in. (50 cm) from the end of the yarn and, using the **thumb cast-on method** **2** and US 6 (4mm) needles, cast on 30 sts.

ROW 1: Knit (k) **3**.
Rep row 1 until 50 rows have been worked.

Bind (cast) off **7**.

Measure the swatch **8**.
Counting rows and stitches **4**. There should be 21 stitches and 39 rows to 4 in. (10 cm).

Making the backpack
Bag

Make a slip knot 22 in. (56 cm) from the end of the yarn and, using the thumb cast-on method and US 6 (4mm) needles, cast on 56 sts.

ROWS 1–10: Knit.

The numbers in the squares refer to instructions in the Workshop sections.

ROW 11: Change to US 10 (6mm) needles and knit.
Knit the row with a US 10 (6mm) needle in the right hand, transferring the stitches from the US 6 (4mm) needle in the left hand.

Then work the next row with two US 10 (6 mm) needles.

ROW 12 : K4, **Knit two stitches together (k2tog) 11**, **yarnover (yo) 12**, [k3, k2tog, yo] nine times, k5.

Rep row 14 until the work measures 26 in. (65 cm) from cast-on edge, ending on a WS row.
The tail of thread from the cast-on will be on the left-hand side of the work.

ROW 13: Change to US 6 (4mm) needles and knit to first yo. Put needle through the yo loop in the same direction as for a knit stitch and knit it. Cont to end of row.
Knit the row with a US 6 (4mm) needle in the right hand, transferring the stitches from the US 10 (6mm) needle in the left hand.

Rep rows 11-13.

Knit 10 rows.

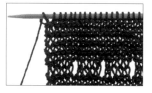

Bind (cast) off.

ROW 14: Using US 6 (4mm) needles, knit.

Straps (make 2)

Make a slip knot 6 in. (15 cm) from the end of the yarn and, using the thumb cast-on method and US 6 (4mm) needles, cast on 8 sts.

ROW 1: Knit.

Rep row 1 until work measures 25½ in. (65 cm). Bind (cast) off.

Finishing

Following the instructions on the ball band, wash all the pieces of knitting. Wash some extra yarn for sewing—placing it in an old pillowcase to prevent it from tangling in the washing machine.

Weave in ends 6 .
Fold the bag piece in half, RS facing and aligning the eyelets. Using **flat stitch 14** , sew the sides together, leaving a gap the width of the eyelets and in line with them.

Lay the straps flat and without stretching them, pin a length of ribbon to each one. The ribbon should protrude ½ in. (1 cm) beyond the ends of each strap. Turn the ends of the ribbon under so that they align with the knitting. Slip-stitch the ribbon to the knitting with blue sewing thread.

Take the strap out through the next hole and weave it in and out of the holes along one side of the bag until it emerges from the opposite gap in the seam.

Making sure that the strap doesn't become twisted, sew the other end of it to the outside bottom corner of the bag below the gap it came out of.

Sew one end of one strap to the stitches beside the gap in a side seam. The knitted side of the strap must face the WS of the bag.

Rep the process with the other strap, sewing it to the stitches beside the gap that the first strap is coming out of. Weave it in and out across the other side of the bag and sew it to the opposite bottom corner. Pull the straps in opposite directions to close the bag.

The numbers in the squares refer to instructions in the Workshop sections.

37

Knit and purl

Workshop

The second basic knitting stitch is the purl stitch. Stockinette (stocking) stitch is created by purling on the back side of a row of knit stitches. This section also introduces the cable cast-on method and some knitted textures, including a simple cable pattern.

You will need

Any durable yarn can be used. Check the manufacturer's band for information on the suggested needle sizes and if a range is suggested, choose the middle size.
The yarn and needles used for the practice swatches in this book are:

Rowan All Seasons Cotton 1¾oz (50g)

1 pair US 7 (4.5mm) needles

Gauge (tension)

The gauge (tension) does not matter too much at this stage; just concentrate on achieving a comfortable flow that will keep the stitches even.

15 Cable cast-on method

This cast on gives a neat edge which is firmer than that of the thumb cast-on method.

1 Create a slip knot and put it on a needle. Hold the needle in the left hand.

2 Insert the right-hand needle into it and wrap the yarn around the right-hand needle as if to knit. Draw the loop through the slip knot.

3 Place the loop onto the left-hand needle.

4 For the third stitch and all subsequent stitches, insert the right-hand needle between the last two stitches before creating a loop and placing it on the left-hand needle.

To practice this stitch

Cast on 15 sts using the cable cast-on method.

The numbers in the squares refer to instructions in the Workshop sections.

39

16 Purl stitch (p)

This is the second most important stitch in knitting.

1 Hold the needle with the cast-on stitches in the left hand and an empty needle in the right hand. Holding the yarn in front of the needle, insert the needle from right to left into the first stitch.

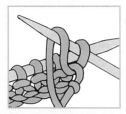

2 Wrap the yarn around the tip of the right-hand needle, going over the top of the needle.

3 Draw the loop just made through the stitch on the left-hand needle.

4 Slide the stitch off the left-hand needle, keeping the new loop on the right-hand needle.

5 Repeat these four steps for each stitch on the left-hand needle.

To practice this stitch

Cast on 15 sts using the **cable cast-on method 15**. For this swatch continue until 27 rows have been completed.
Bind (cast) off 19.

17 Stockinette (stocking) stitch (St st)

This stitch pattern is a combination of alternate knit and purl rows.

To practice this stitch

Cast on 15 sts using the **cable cast-on method 15**.
ROW 1: **Knit (k) 3**.
ROW 2: **Purl (p) 16**.
Repeat rows 1–2 until 20 rows have been worked.

The two sides look different.

This side is known as stockinette (stocking) stitch (St st).
This is often called the right side (RS), and odd-number rows will look like this if the first row is a knit row.

This side is known as **reverse stockinette (stocking) stitch (rev St st).**
This is often called the wrong side (WS) and even-number rows will look like this if the first row is a knit row.

18 Counting rows and stitches

In order to determine the gauge (tension) it is necessary to count the rows and stitches. In the swatch below, the first row after the cast-on row has been knitted in a contrasting color. From this it is possible to see that one row of loops equals one row. When counting rows for a pattern, you do not count the cast-on row, but you do count the row of stitches that is on the needle.

To count the number of stitches, either make a note while the stitches are still on the needle or study the image to the right, which shows one stitch knitted in a contrasting color.

Gauge (tension)

Determining the gauge (tension) is the same as **measuring the swatch** 8. If the yarn and needles specified are used for this swatch, then the gauge (tension) should be 11 stitches and 16 rows to 2 in. (5 cm).

19 Bind (cast) off

The basic principle of binding (casting) off is to work two stitches in the pattern set and to pass the stitch farthest from the tip of the needle over the other one and off the needle.

Bind (cast) off on a knit row

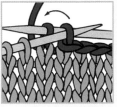

1 Knit two stitches. Insert the left-hand needle into the stitch farthest from the tip of the right-hand needle. Pass this stitch over the first stitch and drop it off both needles.

2 Knit another stitch and repeat as before. Repeat until one stitch remains and fasten off.

Bind (cast) off on a purl row

1 Work as above, but substitute a purl stitch for every knit command.

To practice this stitch

Bind (cast) off the swatch used to practice the stockinette (stocking) stitch (St st).

20 Purl two stitches together (p2tog)

Purling two stitches together is very similar to knitting two stitches together (see k2tog 11, page 16).

1 Position the right-hand needle right to left through the first stitch, and then through the second stitch. Purl the two stitches together in the same way as purling one.

The numbers in the squares refer to instructions in the Workshop sections.

41

21 Rib

This stitch pattern combines knit and purl stitches in vertical strips of stockinette (stocking) stitch and reverse stockinette (stocking) stitch. This pattern is very elastic and to complement this, the thumb cast-on method is often used.

To practice rib (k2, p2)

Cast on 16 sts using the **cable cast-on method 15**.
ROW 1: [**Knit (k) 3** 2 sts, bring the yarn forward between the needles, **purl (p) 16** 2 sts, take the yarn back between the needles] rep the sequence within the brackets to the end of the row.
Rep row 1 until 20 rows have been worked.
On the second row and all even-numbered rows, the knit stitches are worked into what were the purl stitches on the first row.
Bind (cast) off 19, knitting or purling the stitches as required in the patt set.

To practice narrow rib (k1, p1)

Cast on 16 sts using the **cable cast-on method 15**.
ROW 1: [**Knit (k) 3** 1 st, bring the yarn forward between the needles, **purl (p) 16** 1 st, take the yarn back between the needles] repeat the sequence within the brackets to the end of the row.
Rep row 1 until 20 rows have been worked.
On the second row and all even-numbered rows, the knit stitches are worked into what

were the purl stitches on the first row.
Bind (cast) off 19, knitting or purling the stitches as required in the patt set.

22 Seed (moss) stitch

This pattern uses the technique of rib, but with alternate knit and purl stitches from row to row.

To practice seed (moss) stitch

Cast on 15 sts using the **cable cast-on method 15**.
ROW 1: Taking the yarn forward and backwards between the needles as for rib [**knit (k) 3** 1 st, **purl (p) 16** 1 st] repeat the sequence within the brackets until 1 st remains, k1.
Repeat row 1 until 20 rows have been worked.
Bind (cast) off 19, knitting or purling the stitches as required in the patt set.

23 Slip one, knit one, pass the slipped stitch over (skpo)

This decrease slants in the opposite direction compared to knitting two stitches together.

1 Knit to the point of decrease, **slip 1 knitwise (sl1 kwise) 9 .**
Knit the next stitch.

2 Pass the slipped stitch over the knit stitch as if to bind (cast) off.

24 Purl one, pass the next stitch over (ppno)

This decrease slants in the opposite direction to purling two stitches together.

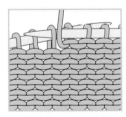

Purl one stitch, pass the stitch back onto the left-hand needle and pass the next stitch on the left-hand needle over the stitch just purled. Put purled st back onto right-hand needle.

To practice these stitches

Cast on 16 sts using the **cable cast-on method 15** .

ROW 1: Knit (k) 3 1 st, **slip one, knit one, pass the slipped stitch over (skpo)**, knit to the end of the row.
(15 sts on the needle.)

ROW 2: Purl (p) 16 .

ROW 3: K1, skpo, knit to the end of the row.
(14 sts on the needle.)

ROW 4: Purl until 3 sts are left on the left-hand needle, **purl one, pass the next stitch over (ppno)**, p1.
(13 sts on the needle.)

ROW 5: K1, skpo, knit to the end of the row.
(12 sts on the needle.)

ROW 6: Purl.

Repeat the last four rows for 12 rows. With each repeat the number of stitches decreases by 3.
(3 sts on the needle.)

ROW 19: Skpo, k1.
(2 sts on the needle.)

ROW 20: Skpo.

Cut the yarn and draw the end through the loop of the last stitch.

To create a square, repeat this swatch and sew the diagonal edges together.

The numbers in the squares refer to instructions in the Workshop sections.

43

25 Increase (inc)

This increase in the number of stitches is created by working a stitch twice and does not result in the hole associated with yarnover. It is, however, not invisible and a small bar appears in front of the stitch.

On a knit row

Knit into the stitch as normal, but do not take the stitch off the left-hand needle. Knit into the same stitch again, but put the right-hand needle through the back of the stitch from right to left before wrapping the yarn around the needle. Draw the loop through and slip the stitch off the left-hand needle. There should now be an extra stitch on the right-hand needle.

On a purl row

Purl into the stitch as normal but do not take the stitch off the left-hand needle. Purl into the same stitch again but put the right-hand needle through the back of the stitch from back to front before wrapping the yarn around the needle. Draw the loop through and slip the stitch off the left-hand needle. There should now be an extra stitch on the right-hand needle.

To practice this stitch

Cast on 15 sts using the **cable cast-on method** 15.

ROW 1: **Knit (k)** 3.

ROW 2: On this and all even-numbered rows, **purl (p)** 16.

ROW 3: K1, **increase (inc)**, **slip one, knit one, pass the slipped stitch over (skpo)** 23, k7, **knit two stitches together (k2tog)** 11, inc, k1.

ROW 5: K2, inc, skpo, k5, k2tog, inc, k2.

ROW 7: K3, inc, skpo, k3, k2tog, inc, k3.

ROW 9: K4, inc, skpo, k1, k2tog, inc, k4.

ROW 11: Knit.

ROW 13: K4, k2tog, inc, k1, inc, skpo, k4.

ROW 15: K3, k2tog, inc, k3, inc, skpo, k3.

ROW 17: K2, k2tog, inc, k5, inc, skpo, k2.

ROW 19: K1, k2tog, inc, k7, inc, skpo, k1.

ROW 20: Purl.

Bind (cast) off 19.

26 Make one (m1)

This increase creates a new stitch between two existing stitches.

1 Insert the right-hand needle from front to back into the loop between the two stitches and lift the loop.

2 Place the loop from front to back onto the left-hand needle. Knit into the back of the loop.

To practice this stitch

Cast on 15 sts using the **cable cast-on method 15**.
ROW 1: **Knit (k) 3**.
ROW 2: **Purl (p) 16**.
ROW 3: K5, **make one (m1)**, **slip one, knit one, pass the slipped stitch over (skpo) 23**, k1, m1, skpo, k5.
ROW 4: Purl.
Rep rows 3–4 eight times.
Bind (cast) off 19.

27 Buttonhole

Buttonholes are a useful technique to master.

1 Bind (cast) off the number of stitches directed in the pattern and continue along the row.

2 On the next row work up to the bound (cast) off stitches. Turn the work around and cast on the same number of stitches as were bound (cast) off using the **cable cast-on method 15**.

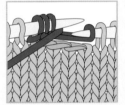

3 Before the last cast-on loop is placed on the left-hand needle, bring the yarn forward between the needles and pull firmly. Turn the work around again and proceed along the row.

To practice buttonholes

Cast on 15 sts using the **cable cast-on method 15**.
ROW 1: **Knit (k) 3**.
ROW 2: **Purl (p) 16**.
These two rows form the **stockinette (stocking) stitch (St st) 17** pattern. Continue in St st until 8 rows have been completed.
BUTTONHOLE ROW 1: K6, **bind (cast) off 19** 3 sts, knit the next 5 sts.
BUTTONHOLE ROW 2: P6 and complete the buttonhole. Turn the work around and p6. Continue in St st until 8 rows more have been completed.
Bind (cast) off 19.

The numbers in the squares refer to instructions in the Workshop sections.

45

28 Cable

Cable is a texture created by changing the order in which stitches are knitted with the aid of a cable needle. In cable back, stitches are passed behind other stitches. In cable front, stitches are passed in front of other stitches. The number of stitches to be moved will be stated in the pattern.

Cable back

1 Put the number of stitches stated onto a cable needle.

2 Position the cable needle at the back of the work and knit the stated number of stitches from the left-hand needle.

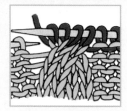

3 Bring the cable needle to the front of the work and knit the stitches on it.

Cable front

Cable front differs only in that the stitches slipped onto the cable needle are held at the front of the work while the stitches are knitted from the left-hand needle.

To practice this stitch

Cable 4 back (c4b): Slip 2 sts onto the cable needle and hold at the back of the work. Knit 2 sts from the left-hand needle, then the 2 from the cable needle.

Cast on 19 sts using the **cable cast-on method 15**.
ROW 1: Purl (p) 16 4 sts, **knit (k) 3** 4 sts, p3, k4, p4.
ROW 2: K4, p4, k3, p4, k4.
ROW 3: P4, **cable four back (c4b)**, p3, c4b, p4.
ROW 4: K4, p4, k3, p4, k4.
ROW 5: P4, k4, p3, k4, p4.
ROW 6: K4, p4, k3, p4, k4.
Repeat the last 6 rows twice more.
(Total 18 rows)
Bind (cast) off 19.

29 Mattress stitch

This technique produces a discreet seam that is especially good if the edge stitches are not very neat, as they become part of the seam inside the project. The other advantage of mattress stitch is that it is worked from the right side, so the neatness of the seam can be assessed as the seam is stitched and adjustments made immediately, rather than having to painstakingly unpick a whole seam.

Careful preparation will pay dividends, so press and block the pieces first, paying particular attention to the edge stitches. Then pin the seam.

Between two knit stitches along the sides

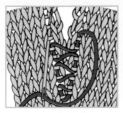

Working from the bottom, and between the first and second stitch in from the edge, pass the needle under the loops of two rows on one side; then pass the needle under the loops of the corresponding two rows on other side. Work a few stitches like this before drawing the first stitches tight as this will help to keep track of the line of the seam. The neatest seam is achieved by pulling the yarn just enough to pull the stitches together.

Between two purl stitches or garter stitch along the sides

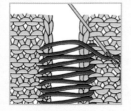

Each ridge of stitches has an upper loop and a lower loop in a wave-like structure. Working from the bottom, pass the needle under the upper loop on one side and the lower loop of the corresponding row on the other side.

Between sides and top or bottom edges

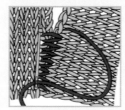

Bring the needle up through the middle of the top or bottom edge stitches and pick up one loop between the first and second stitch in from the edge. Then sew back down through the middle of the first stitch and come up again through the middle of the adjacent stitch. Repeat along the seam.

Between bound (cast) off or cast-on edges

Bring the needle up through the middle of the first stitch on the lower edge. Pass the needle behind the corresponding stitch on the upper edge. Then sew down through the middle of the first stitch on the lower edge and up through the middle of the adjacent stitch. Repeat along the seam.

To practice this stitch

Use the swatches in this chapter to practice these seam techniques.

The numbers in the squares refer to instructions in the Workshop sections.

Heart cushion

A stylish introduction to stockinette (stocking) stitch, this cushion is made up of separate panels of color, so there is no complicated color knitting required.

Size

Cushion insert size: 16 × 16 in. (40 × 40 cm)

You will need

3½oz (100g) balls of Rowan DK Cotton
  Four in light blue (A)
  One in cream (B)
  Three in pink (C)

⅝ in. (20mm) buttons
  Nine light blue
  Five pink

US 6 (4mm) needles
Tapestry needle

Gauge (tension) swatch

Using yarn A and the **cable cast-on method** 🔢, cast on 30 sts.

ROW 1: **Knit (k)** 🔢.

ROW 2: **Purl (p)** 🔢.

Rep rows 1–2 until 40 rows have been worked.

Bind (cast) off 🔢.

Measure the swatch 🔢.
Counting rows and stitches 🔢. There should be 19 stitches and 24 rows to 4 in. (10cm).

The numbers in the squares refer to instructions in the Workshop sections.

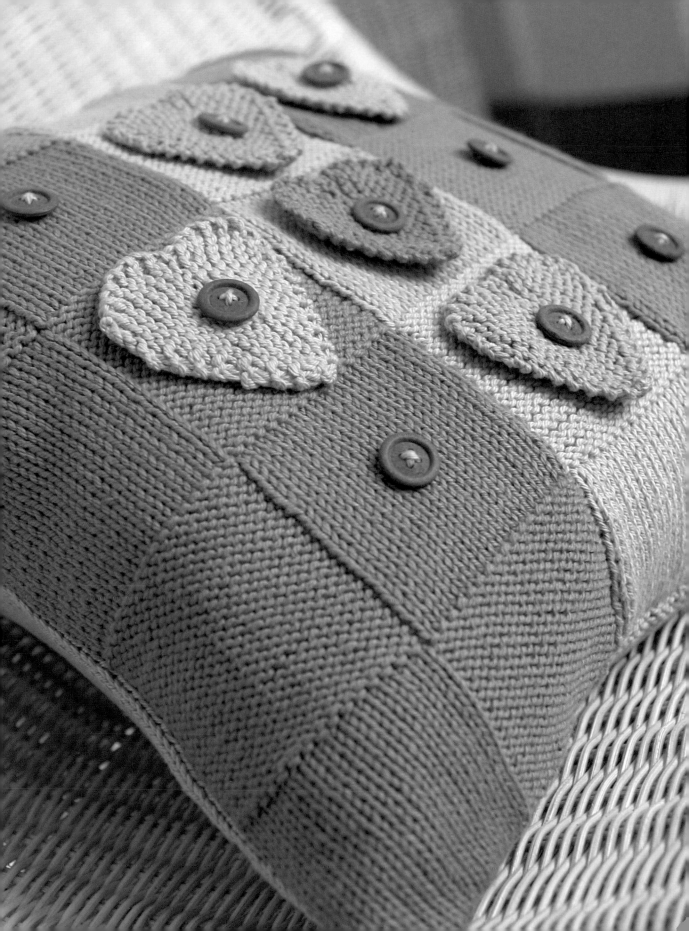

Front
Center front

Using yarn B and the cable cast-on method, cast on 19 sts.

ROW 1: Knit.

ROW 2: Purl.

Rep rows 1–2 until 22 rows have been worked.

ROW 23: Purl.

ROW 24: Knit.

Rep rows 23–24 until 44 rows have been worked.

ROW 45: Knit.

ROW 46: Purl.

Rep rows 45–46 until 66 rows have been worked.

Rep rows 23–66 once more until 110 rows have been worked.

Bind (cast) off.

Right front

Using yarn A and the cable cast-on method, cast on 36 sts.

ROW 1: K18, bring the yarn forward between the needles, p18.

ROW 2: K18, bring the yarn forward between the needles, p18.

Rep row 2 until 22 rows have been worked.

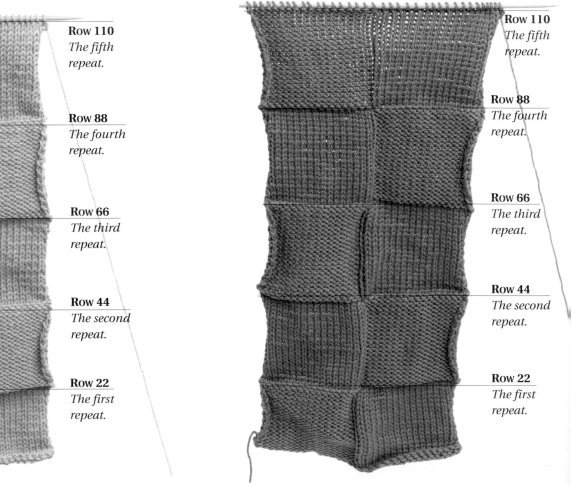

Row 110
The fifth repeat.

Row 88
The fourth repeat.

Row 66
The third repeat.

Row 44
The second repeat.

Row 22
The first repeat.

Row 110
The fifth repeat.

Row 88
The fourth repeat.

Row 66
The third repeat.

Row 44
The second repeat.

Row 22
The first repeat.

ROW 23: P18, take the yarn back between the needles, k18.

ROW 24: P18, take the yarn back between the needles, k18.

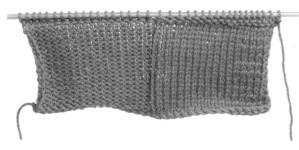

Rep row 24 until 44 rows have been worked.

ROW 45: K18, bring the yarn forward between the needles, p18.

ROW 46: K18, bring the yarn forward between the needles, p18.

Rep row 46 until 66 rows have been worked.

Rep rows 23–66 once more until 110 rows have been worked.

Bind (cast) off.

Left front

This is a mirror image of the Right Front.

Using yarn A and the cable cast-on method, cast on 36 sts.

ROW 1: P18, k18.

Rep row 1 until 22 rows have been worked.

ROW 23: K18, p18.

Rep row 23 until 44 rows have been worked.

ROW 45: P18, k18.

Rep row 45 until 66 rows have been worked.

Rep rows 23–66 once more until 110 rows have been worked.

Bind (cast) off.

Back flap
Center back flap

Using yarn B and the cable cast-on method, cast on 19 sts.

ROW 1: Knit.

ROW 2: Purl.

ROW 3: K8, bind (cast) off 3 sts to make the buttonhole, k7.
(8 sts + 8 sts)

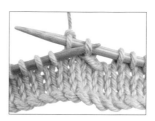

ROW 4: P8, complete the **buttonhole 27**, p8.

Work as for Center Front from row 5 to row 44.
Bind (cast) off.

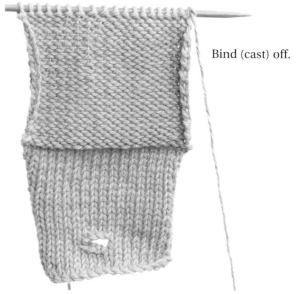

Bind (cast) off.

The numbers in the squares refer to instructions in the Workshop sections.

51

Right back flap

Using yarn A and the cable cast-on method, cast on 36 sts.

ROW 1: K18, bring the yarn forward between the needles, p18.

ROW 2: K18, take the yarn forward between the needles, p18.

ROW 3: K8, bind (cast) off 3 sts, k6, bring the yarn forward between the needles, p7, bind (cast) off 3 sts purlwise, p7.

ROW 4: K8, complete buttonhole, k7, bring the yarn forward between the needles, p7, complete buttonhole, p8.

Work as for Right Front from row 5 to row 44.

Bind (cast) off.

Left back flap

This is a mirror image of the Right Back Flap.

Using yarn A and the cable cast-on method, cast on 36 sts.

ROW 1: P18, take the yarn back between the needles, k18.

ROW 2: P18, take the yarn back between the needles, k18.

ROW 3: P8, bind (cast) off 3 sts purlwise, p6, take the yarn back between the needles, k7, bind (cast) off 3 sts, k7.

ROW 4: P8, complete buttonhole, p7, take the yarn back between the needles, k7, complete buttonhole, k8.

Work as for left front from row 5 to row 44.

Bind (cast) off.

Back panel

Using yarn C and the cable cast-on method, cast on 87 sts.

ROW 1 (RS): K35, bring the yarn forward between the needles, p17, take the yarn back between the needles, k35.

ROW 2: P35, take the yarn back between the needles, k17, bring the yarn forward between the needles, p35.

Rep rows 1–2 until 76 rows have been worked. End with a WS row.

Bind (cast) off.

Heart (make two in each color)

Knit this heart shape quite tightly. It may curl slightly, but blocking will make it lie flat.

Make a **slip knot** ❶ 4 in. (10 cm) from the end of the yarn C and, using the **thumb cast-on method** ❷, cast on 3 sts.

 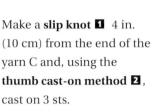

ROW 1: K1, **increase (inc)** ㉕ into next st,

K1.

(There are now 4 sts on the needle.)

ROW 2: K1, inc, inc, k1.
(6 sts)

ROW 3: K4, inc, k1.

ROW 4: K1, inc, knit to last 2 sts, inc, k1.
(9 sts)

ROW 5: Knit to last 2 sts, inc, k1.

ROW 6: K1, inc, knit to last 2 sts, inc, k1.
(12 sts)

ROW 7: Knit to last 2 sts, inc, k1.

ROW 8: K1, inc, knit to end of row.

Rep rows 7–8 twice more.
(18 sts)

ROW 13: K1, **knit two stitches together (k2tog)** ⓫, knit to last 2 sts, inc, k1.
(18 sts)

ROW 14: K1, inc, knit to last 3 sts, k2tog, k1.
(18 sts)

ROW 15: K2tog, k1, k2tog, k3, bind (cast) off 3 sts, knit to last 3 sts, inc, k1, inc.
(6 sts + 9 sts)

ROW 16: K2tog, k7, turn work, cast on 3 sts to complete the buttonhole, knit to end of row.
(17 sts)

The numbers in the squares refer to instructions in the Workshop sections.

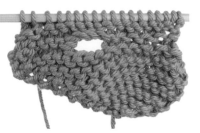

ROW 17: Inc, k1, inc, knit to last 3 sts, k2tog, k1.

(18 sts)

ROW 18: K1, k2tog, knit to last 2 sts, inc, k1.

ROW 19: Knit to last 3 sts, k2tog, k1.

ROW 20: K1, k2tog, knit to end of row.

Rep rows 19–20 for four more rows.

(12 sts)

ROW 25: Knit to last 3 sts, k2tog, k1.

ROW 26: K1, k2tog, knit to last 3 sts, k2tog, k1.

ROW 27: Knit to last 3 sts, k2tog, k1.

ROW 28: K1, k2tog, knit to last 3 sts, k2tog, k1.

ROW 29: Knit to last 3 sts, k2tog, k1.

(5 sts)

ROW 30: K1, [k2tog, pass the first st on the right-hand needle over the second stitch] twice.

(1 st)

Cut the yarn and pull it through the last stitch knitted.

Finishing

Block and press 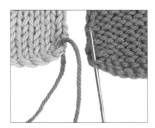 the pieces gently. Take particular care with the edges, as this will make sewing up easier. Sew the pieces together using **mattress stitch** 29. Cut a length of yarn from the ball and thread the tapestry needle.

Start by laying the center back flap and the right back flap pieces right-sides up and with the cast-on edges at the bottom.

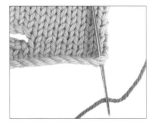

Leaving a 4 in. (10 cm) tail, bring the needle from back to front through the bottom loop on the right-hand edge of the left piece.

Rep this on the left-hand edge of the right piece.

On the stockinette (stocking) stitch edge, insert the needle between the first and second stitch and pick up two loops.

On the reverse stockinette (stocking) stitch edge, insert the needle under the second upper loop of one row of stitches.

Rep these two steps and cont sewing up the seam, reversing the process as the pattern textures change.

Pull the starting tail of yarn tight and weave it into the seam.

In the same manner, attach the left back flap piece to the left of the center flap piece.
Rep with the front pieces to create the front panel.

Attach the bound (cast) off edge of the back flap to the cast-on edge of the front.
With the pieces right-sides up, bring the needle up, from back to front, through the outer stitch loops on the top and bottom edges.

Attach the cast-on edge of the back panel to the bound (cast) off edge of the front panel in the same way.

Fold the back panels to the back and sew the lower back side seams using mattress stitch on stockinette (stocking) stitch and reverse stockinette (stocking) stitch as required. Put in the cushion insert.

Sew the back flap panel to the front. Start at the fold and, using mattress stitch, sew two-thirds of the depth of the flap to the front.

Sew the pink buttons to the back panel to align with the buttonholes on the back flap panel.
Sew the blue buttons to the front panel, positioning them in the middle of the nine center squares.
Weave in ends 6 into the seams.
Button the hearts onto the front panel as desired.

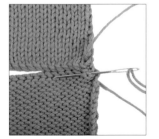

On the reverse stockinette (stocking) stitch edge, insert the needle between the top and second ridge of stitches, picking up two loops.

On the stockinette (stocking) stitch edge, insert the needle behind one stitch loop.

The numbers in the squares refer to instructions in the Workshop sections.

55

Rabbit

This crouching rabbit is soft and tactile, as well as simple to knit. It mixes garter stitch and stockinette (stocking) stitch to good effect.

Size

Nose to tail: 9 in. (23 cm)

You will need

Two 3½oz (100g) balls of Rowan Yorkshire Tweed Aran in light brown

US 10½ (6.5mm) needles
Tapestry needle
Stuffing
Short length of dark brown wool yarn

Gauge (tension) swatch

Using the **cable cast-on method** 15, cast on 30 sts.

ROW 1: **Knit (k)** 3.

ROW 2: **Purl (p)** 16.
Rep rows 1–2 until 40 rows have been worked.

Bind (cast) off 19.

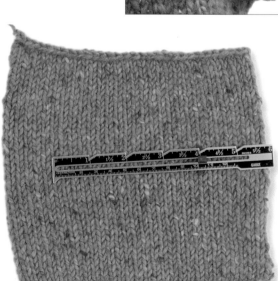

Measure the swatch 8.
Counting rows and stitches 18. There should be 16 sts and 26 rows to 4 in. (10 cm).

The numbers in the squares refer to instructions in the Workshop sections.

Making the rabbit
Body (make 3)

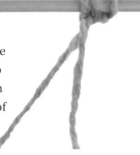

Make a **slip knot** **1** 4 in. (10 cm) from the end of the yarn and, using the **thumb cast-on method** **2**, cast on 3 sts (this is the nose end of the rabbit's body).

ROW 1: Purl.

ROW 2: Increase (inc) 25 in first st,

knit to last st, inc in last st.

(5 sts)

Rep rows 1–2 nine times more.

(23 sts)

ROW 21: Purl.

ROW 22: Knit.

ROW 23: Purl.

ROW 24: Inc in first st, knit to last st, inc in last st.

Rep rows 21–24 three times more.

(31 sts)

ROW 37: Purl.

ROW 38: Knit.

Rep rows 37–38 seven times more.

ROW 53: Purl.

ROW 54: knit two stitches together (k2tog) 11, knit to last 2 sts, k2tog.

(29 sts)

Rep rows 53–54 four times more.

(21 sts)

ROW 63: **Purl two stitches together (p2tog)** [20], purl to last 2 sts, p2tog.

ROW 64: K2tog, knit to last 2 sts, k2tog.

Ears (make 2)

Make a slip knot 12 in. (30 cm) from the end of the yarn and, using the thumb cast-on method, cast on 20 sts.

ROW 1: **Slip 1 knitwise (sl1 kwise)** [9], knit to end of row.

Rep row 1 until 60 rows have been worked.

Rep rows 63–64 three times more, then rep row 63 once more.

(3 sts)

Bind (cast) off [19].

Repeat twice more for a total of three body pieces.

ROW 61: K2tog,

knit to last 2 sts, k2tog. Rep row 61 eight times more.

(2 sts)

ROW 89: K2tog.

The numbers in the squares refer to instructions in the Workshop sections.

Cut the yarn leaving a 30 in. (80 cm) tail. Thread the tail through the last st and pull it up tightly. Make a second ear.

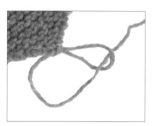

Tail

Wind yarn around four fingers about thirty times.

Take the bundle of yarn off the fingers and tie it firmly in the middle with another length of yarn.

Cut through the ends of the bundle with sharp scissors.

Fluff up the bundle and trim the ends to make a round pom-pom. Trim only one of the tails of the yarn used to bind the bundle; leave the other one long.

Finishing

Gently **block and press** 🔢 the body and ear pieces.

Lay two body pieces side by side, with the pointed nose ends together. Using **mattress stitch** 🔢, sew the pieces together.

Lay the third body piece nose-to-nose along the free edge of one of the two joined pieces and sew the edges together. Sew the remaining two edges together, leaving a small gap. Stuff the rabbit's body quite firmly and finish sewing the seam.

Weave the 30 in. (80 cm) tail of yarn left from binding (casting) off up the side of the ear through the stitches so that it appears at one of the top corners.

Fold an ear so that it has a pleat in the middle. Using the same tail of yarn, sew the ear to the rabbit's body, positioning it as shown. Rep the process with the other ear and its tail of yarn on the other side of the body.

Using the long tail of yarn, sew the pom-pom to the rabbit's bottom.

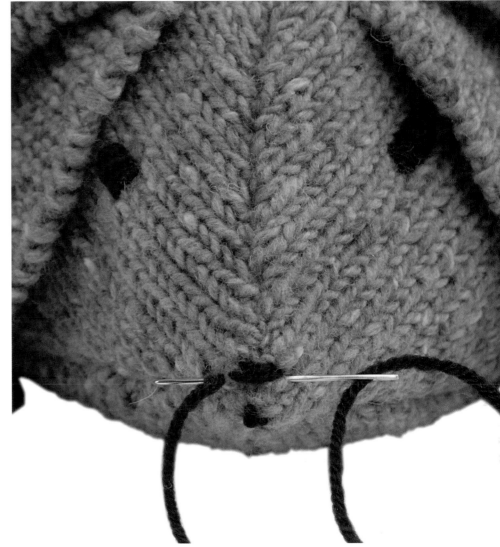

Using the dark brown yarn, embroider eyes and a nose on the rabbit's face. Thread the needle, make a knot in the yarn and trim the end very close to the knot. To secure the end of the yarn, take the needle through a stitch that will be covered by the embroidery and pull it through up to the knot.

The numbers in the squares refer to instructions in the Workshop sections.

Pom-pom scarf

Though this scarf is worked in rib, it is short and therefore quite quick to make. One pom-pom tucks through the slit to hold it in place around your neck.

Size

4¾ × 35½ in. (12 × 90 cm)

You will need

Two 1¾oz (50g) balls of Rowan Wool Cotton
    in bright green
One 1¾oz (50g) ball of Rowan Wool Cotton
    in turquoise

US 6 (4mm) needles
2 small stitch holders
Tapestry needle
3 × 6 in. (7.5 × 15 cm) piece of thick cardboard
Compass
Small, sharp scissors

Gauge (tension) swatch

Make a **slip knot** **1** 24 in. (60 cm) from the end of the green yarn and, using the **thumb cast-on method** **2**, cast on 45 sts.

ROW 1: [**Knit (k)** **3** 1 st,   **purl (p)** **16** 1 st] rep to last st, k1.

ROW 2: [P1, k1] to last st, p1.
These 2 rows make the **rib** **21** pattern (patt). *For the first few rows you need to be careful to make the correct stitch, but after a few rows the patt is established and it becomes easier to see and to work.*

Rep rows 1–2 until 40 rows have been worked. **Bind (cast) off** **19** .

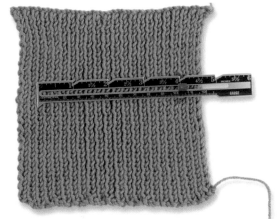

Measure the swatch **8** . **Counting rows and stitches** **18** . There should be 33 stitches and 29 rows to 4 in. (10 cm).

Note: when the rib fabric is lying flat it will close up and the columns of reverse stockinette (stocking) stitch will hardly be visible, but they must be counted as stitches when measuring the swatch.

The numbers in the squares refer to instructions in the Workshop sections.

Making the scarf
Scarf

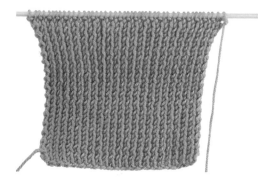

Make a slip knot 24 in. (60 cm) from the end of the green yarn and, using the thumb cast-on method, cast on 45 sts. Do not trim the tail of yarn.

ROW 1: [K1, p1] to last st, k1.

ROW 2: [P1, k1] to last st, p1.

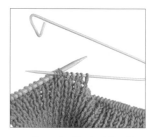

Rep rows 1–2 until 33 rows have been worked.

ROW 34: Work 23 sts in rib. Place the 22 sts remaining on the left-hand needle onto a holder.

Slip the tip of the stitch holder under a few stitches, then slip the stitches off the needle onto the holder. Rep until all the stitches are transferred onto the holder.

ROW 35: Turn the work around and work across the 23 sts on the needles, keeping the rib patt correct.

Cont working in rib on the 23 sts until 21 rows more have been worked, ending on row 56. Slip the 23 stitches onto a stitch holder and break the yarn leaving an 8 in. (20 cm) tail of yarn.

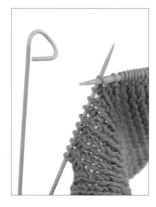

Slip the 22 sts from the first holder back onto a needle.

Slip the tip of the needle under a few stitches; then slip the stitches off the holder onto the needle. Rep until all the stitches are transferred onto the needle.

The stitches need to be facing the other way to start the next row, so, using the same technique, transfer the stitches from one needle onto another.

The first stitch is a knit stitch, so put the right-hand needle through the loop on the left-hand needle in the usual way. Fold a loop of new yarn over the tip of the right-hand needle and pull it through to make the knit stitch. The tail of yarn from the new loop should be 8 in. (20 cm) long.

Bring the yarn and the tail forward between the needles and purl the next stitch, ensuring that you make the stitch with the working yarn, not with the tail.

Work across the row, keeping the rib patt correct.

Cont working in rib on the 22 sts until 22 rows more have been completed.

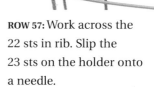

ROW 57: Work across the 22 sts in rib. Slip the 23 sts on the holder onto a needle.

Work across the 23 sts, keeping the rib patt correct.

Cont working in rib until the work measures 32 in. (80 cm) long.

Bind (cast) off, leaving a long tail of yarn.

The numbers in the squares refer to instructions in the Workshop sections.

Pom-poms (make 2)

Using the compass, draw two 2½ in. (6 cm) diameter circles on the cardboard. Draw a central 1¼ in. (3 cm) diameter circle inside each one. Cut out the circles with scissors.

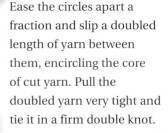

Ease the circles apart a fraction and slip a doubled length of yarn between them, encircling the core of cut yarn. Pull the doubled yarn very tight and tie it in a firm double knot.

Cut off approximately 40 yds (37 m) of turquoise yarn. Place one circle on top of the other and wind yarn around them tightly and evenly until all the yarn is used.

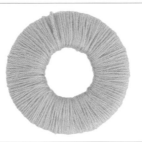

Fluff up the pom-pom and trim any protruding ends with the scissors.

Slip the points of the scissors into the wound yarn and between the circles of cardboard. Snip around the edge of the circles, snipping through all the layers of yarn.

Finishing

Weave in ends  at either end of the split. Weave them up and down a row rather than across the stitches.

If the ends of the split are a little loose, you can use the tails of yarn to reinforce them by weaving the tails in around the loose stitch.

Using the long tails of yarn left from casting on and binding (casting) off, and the tapestry needle, work running stitches across the ends of the scarf and gather them up tightly. Secure them by oversewing the gathers.

Trim all but one of the tails of yarn extending from the pom-poms. Using the remaining tail and the tapestry needle, tightly sew the pom-poms to the ends of the scarf.

The numbers in the squares refer to instructions in the Workshop sections.

Pom-pom hat

This hat is designed to complement the Pom-pom scarf on page 62. However, you don't need to make the scarf in order to knit this project.

Size

Measure the head around the widest part across the forehead.

Large head size: 22½ in. (57 cm).

Knitted hat circumference (not stretched):
    19½ in. (50 cm).

You will need

One 1¾oz (50g) balls of Rowan Wool Cotton in turquoise

One 1¾oz (50g) ball of Rowan Wool Cotton in bright green

US 5 (3.75mm) and US 6 (4mm) needles

Tapestry needle

3 × 6 in. (7.5 × 15 cm) piece of thick cardboard

Compass

Small, sharp scissors

Gauge (tension) swatch

If you are making the scarf, then use the same gauge (tension) swatch. If you are not knitting the scarf, then knit a swatch following the instructions on page 63.

Making the hat

Make a **slip knot** ◼1 53 in. (135 cm) from the end of the turquoise yarn and, using the **thumb cast-on method** ◼2 and US 5 (3.75mm) needles, cast on 131 sts.

Following the instructions for **rib** ◼21 on page 64, work k1, p1 rib until 24 rows have been worked.

Change to US 6 (4mm) needles.

ROW 25: **Knit (k)** ◼3.

ROW 26: **Purl (p)** ◼16.

Rep rows 25–26 until 16 rows more of **stockinette (stocking) stitch (St st)** ◼17, have been worked.

The numbers in the squares refer to instructions in the Workshop sections.

ROW 43: K2, [**knit two stitches together (k2tog) 11. ** k14] eight times, k1. *(123 sts)*

ROW 44: On this and all even-numbered rows, purl.

ROW 45: K2, [k2tog, k13] eight times, k1. *(115 sts)*

ROW 47: K2, [k2tog, k12] eight times, k1. *(107 sts)*

ROW 49: K2, [k2tog, k11] eight times, k1. *(99 sts)*

ROW 51: K2, [k2tog, k10] eight times, k1. *(91 sts)*

ROW 53: K2, [k2tog, k9] eight times, k1. *(83 sts)*

ROW 55: K2, [k2tog, k8] eight times, k1. *(75 sts)*

ROW 57: K2, [k2tog, k7] eight times, k1. *(67 sts)*

ROW 59: K2, [k2tog, k6] eight times, k1. *(59 sts)*

ROW 61: K2, [k2tog, k5] eight times, k1. *(51 sts)*

ROW 63: K2, [k2tog, k4] eight times, k1. *(43 sts)*

ROW 65: K2, [k2tog, k3] eight times, k1. *(35 sts)*

ROW 67: K2, [k2tog, k2] eight times, k1. *(27 sts)*

ROW 69: K2, [k2tog, k1] eight times, k1. *(19 sts)*

ROW 71: K2, k2tog eight times, k1. *(11 sts)*

ROW 72: Purl.

ROW 73: K1, k2tog five times. *(6 sts)*

Bind (cast) off 🔟 purlwise.

Pom-pom
Make one pom-pom in bright green following the instructions on page 66.

Finishing
Weave in ends 🄶.

Right-sides facing, sew up 2½ in. (6 cm) of the rib using **mattress stitch** 🈁. The raw edges of the seam will be on the right side of the hat.

Turn the hat right-side out and bring the needle and yarn through to the right side. Keeping the mattress stitches even, sew up the rest of the rib so that the raw edges of this part of the seam are on the wrong side.

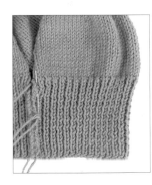

Keeping the hat right-side out, sew up the rest of the seam.

Attach the pom-pom to the top of the hat using the technique described on page 67.

The numbers in the squares refer to instructions in the Workshop sections.

71

Mittens

These mittens are knitted on two needles, rather than the traditional four. They are very easy to customize with either store-bought trimmings and bobbles or with different stitch patterns and color as more knitting techniques are mastered.

Size

Knitted palm circumference at widest point is 9½ in. (24 cm).

Length can be adjusted.

You will need

Three 1¾oz (50g) balls of Rowan Wool Cotton
    in turquoise

US 4 (3.5mm) needles
US 5 (3.75mm) needles
Two stitch holders
Tapestry needle

Gauge (tension) swatch

Make a **slip knot** 🔟 11 in. (28 cm) from the end of the yarn and, using the **thumb cast-on method** 🔟 on US 5 (3.75 mm) needles, cast on 28 sts.

ROW 1: **Knit (k)** 🔟.

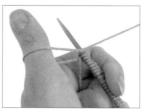

ROW 2: **Purl (p)** 🔟.

Rep rows 1–2 until 22 rows of **stockinette (stocking) stitch (St st)** 🔟 have been worked.

Bind (cast) off 🔟.

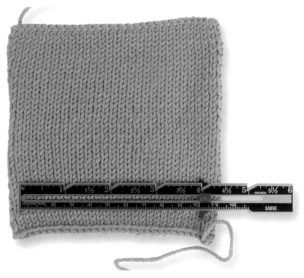

Measure the swatch 🔟.
Counting rows and stitches 🔟. There should be 24 stitches and 18 rows to 4 in. (10 cm).

The numbers in the squares refer to instructions in the Workshop sections.

Right mitten
Cuff

The mitten is knitted from the wrist to the tips of the fingers.

Make a slip knot 25 in. (65 cm) from the end of the yarn and, using the thumb cast-on method and US 4 (3.5mm) needles, cast on 54 sts.
The cuff is worked in a k2, p2 **rib**  pattern (patt).

ROW 1: [K2, p2] rep to the last 2 sts, k2.
ROW 2: [P2, k2] rep to the last 2 sts, p2.
Rep rows 1–2 until 20 rows have been worked.

Use a US 5 (3.75mm) needle in the right hand.

ROW 21: K30, **make one (m1)** .

Knit the remaining 24 stitches of the row.
(55 sts)
Use US 5 (3.75mm) needles in the both hands.
ROW 22: Purl.

Thumb gusset

The number of stitches is increased at this point to accommodate the base of the thumb and the widening of the mitten for the hand.
ROW 23: K30, m1, k1, m1, k24.
(57 sts)
ROW 24: On this and all even-numbered rows, purl.
ROW 25: K30, m1, k3, m1, k24.
ROW 27: K30, m1, k5, m1, k24.
ROW 29: K30, m1, k7, m1, k24.
ROW 31: K30, m1, k9, m1, k24.
ROW 33: K30, m1, k11, m1, k24.
ROW 35: K30, m1, k13, m1, k24.
ROW 37: K30, m1, k15, m1, k24.
ROW 39: K30, m1, k17, m1, k24.
(73 sts)

ROWS 40–43: Work even in St st.

Thumb

Stitches for the hand are put on stitch holders while the thumb is knitted.

ROW 44: P43, put the 30 sts not knitted on this row onto a stitch holder.
Slip the stitches purlwise onto a stitch holder.

The numbers in the squares refer to instructions in the Workshop sections.

Turn the needle with the stitches that have just been purled and hold it as if to knit back along the row.

ROW 45: Cast on 2 sts using the **cable cast-on method** 🇪. Then knit the two cast-on sts and another 19 sts. Transfer the 24 sts not knitted onto a stitch holder as shown before. Turn the work again as if to purl back along the row.

ROW 46: Cast on 2 sts using the cable cast-on method and purl the cast-on stitches and the remaining stitches that are not on either stitch holder.

(23 sts)

ROWS 47-66: Knit the 23 sts in St st for 20 rows, the last row being WS facing.

ROW 67: K2, [k2tog, k1] rep to end of row.

(16 sts)

ROW 68: Purl two stitches together (p2tog) 🄴, rep to end of row.

(8 sts)

Cut the yarn 6 in. (15 cm) from the last stitch and thread a tapestry needle with it.
Slip the stitches purlwise onto the tapestry needle.

Pull tight the last stitch knitted; then draw the stitches together.
Insert the needle through the stitches again to secure them.

Hand

Using a US 5 (3.75mm) needle and with RS facing, slip the stitches purlwise off the right-hand stitch holder. Turn the needle so the WS of the mitten is facing.

ROW 44: Using the second needle, insert it into the first stitch on the left-hand needle as if to purl. Then rejoin the yarn by looping the yarn over the needle, 4 in. (10 cm) from the end. Purl the row.

ROW 45: Knit the stitches on the needle. Turn the needle with the stitches so the WS is facing and cast on 3 sts using the thumb cast-on method and the tail left when the yarn was rejoined.

With WS facing, slip the stitches purlwise from the other stitch holder onto the needle with no stitches on it. Then, RS facing, knit these stitches onto the right-hand needle.
(57 sts)

Cont working all the sts in St st until the mitten measures 2 in. (5 cm) shorter than the desired length. End on a WS row.

Shaping at the top of the glove

Reducing the number of stitches on a row creates shaping. The decreased stitches are positioned to create a distinct shaped edge to the mitten. The shaping starts on a RS knit row.

NEXT ROW: K2, **slip one**

knit one, pass the slipped stitch over (skpo) 🗠,

k22, k2tog, k1, skpo, k22, k2tog, k2.

(53 sts)

NEXT 3 ROWS: Work even in St st.
NEXT ROW: K2, skpo, k20, k2tog, k1, skpo, k20, k2tog, k2.
NEXT 3 ROWS: Work even in St st.
(49 sts)

NEXT ROW: K2, skpo, k18, k2tog, k1, skpo, k18, k2tog, k2.
NEXT ROW: Purl.
NEXT ROW: K2, skpo, k16, k2tog, k1, skpo, k16, k2tog, k2.
NEXT ROW: Purl.
NEXT ROW: K2, skpo, k14, k2tog, k1, skpo, k14, k2tog, k2.
NEXT ROW: Purl.
NEXT ROW: K2, skpo, k12, k2tog, k1, skpo, k12, k2tog, k2.
NEXT ROW: Purl.
(33 sts)

NEXT ROW: K2, skpo, k1, skpo, k7, k2tog, k1, skpo, k7, k2tog, k1, k2tog, k2.
(27 sts)

NEXT ROW: Purl.
Bind (cast) off.

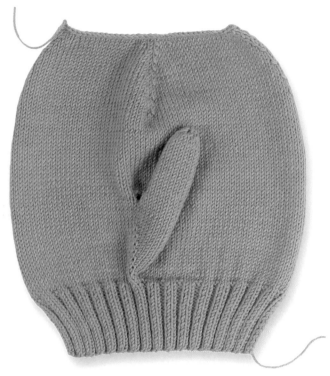

Knit left mitten
Cuff

ROWS 1–22: Work as for Right Mitten.

Thumb gusset

ROW 23: K24, m1, k1, m1, k30.

Compare this row with row 23 of the Right Mitten and notice how the knit 30 sts and knit 24 sts have transposed to create a mirror image of each other. This is called reverse shaping.

Cont with the thumb gusset and thumb following the patt set and using the Right Mitten as reference.

Hand and top of glove

Rejoin the yarn and cont to follow the patt of the Right Mitten with the shaping reversed until row 45.
(57 sts)

Match the number of St st rows to that of Right Mitten. The top shaping is exactly the same for both Right and Left Mitten, as the number of stitches is symmetrical.

Finishing

Block and press  both mittens gently, avoiding the rib. Take particular care with the side edges, as this will make seaming easier.

Thumb

Thread the tail of yarn left at the thumb into the tapestry needle. Sew the sides together using **mattress stitch 29** .

Still using mattress stitch, sew the base of the thumb to the middle cast-on stitch on the main body of the glove. Then work out from the center, securing the thumb to the hand.

Hand

Cut a length of yarn from the ball and thread the tapestry needle. Leaving a 4 in. (10 cm) tail, sew the two side edges together using mattress stitch.

With a new length of yarn, sew the top edges together using mattress stitch. **Weave in ends G** into the seams.

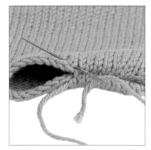

The numbers in the squares refer to instructions in the Workshop sections.

Cable handbag

Though the pattern for this little bag may look rather complex, it is actually quite straightforward to knit. Both sides are the same and are symmetrical, and the cable pattern repeat is over six rows.

Size
Not including handle: 9 × 11 in. (23 × 28 cm)

You will need
Three 1¾oz (50g) balls of Rowan All Seasons Cotton in gray

US 6 (4mm) needles
Cable needle
Tapestry needle

Gauge (tension) swatch

Make a **slip knot** ❶ 20 in. (50 cm) from the end of the yarn and using the **thumb cast-on method** ❷, cast on 38 sts.

ROW 1: **Knit (k)** ❸.

ROW 2: **Purl (p)** ❶❻.

Rep rows 1–2 until 40 rows have been worked.

Bind (cast) off ❶❾.

Measure the swatch ❽.
Counting rows and stitches ❶❽. There should be 18 stitches and 29 rows to 4 in. (10 cm).

The numbers in the squares refer to instructions in the Workshop sections.

Making the bag
Bag (make 2)

Make a slip knot 20 in. (50 cm) from the end of the yarn and using the thumb cast-on method, cast on 38 sts.

ROW 1: [K2,p2], rep to last 2 sts, k2. This is in a k2, p2 **rib** 24 pattern (patt).

ROW 46: P2, [k2, p2] twice, k1,

make one (m1) 26, k1, p2, k2, p2, k1, m1, k1, p2, k2, p2, k1, m1, k1, [p2, k2] twice, p2.
(41 sts)

ROW 47: [K2, p2] twice, k2, p3, k2, p2, k2, p3, k2, p2, k2, p3, k2, [p2, k2] twice.
ROW 48: P2, [k2, p2] twice, k1, m1, k2, p2, k2, p2, k1, m1, k2, p2, k2, p2, k1, m1, k2, [p2, k2] twice, p2.
(44 sts)

ROW 2: [P2, k2], rep to last 2 sts, p2.

ROW 49: [**Increase (inc)** 25 into next 2 sts, p2] twice, inc into next 2 sts, p4, inc into next 2 sts, p2, inc into next 2 sts, p4, inc into next 2 sts, p2, inc into next 2 sts, p4, inc into next 2 sts, [p2, inc into next 2 sts] twice.
(64 sts)

Rep rows 1–2 until 45 rows have been worked.

ROW 50: P16, k4, p10, k4, p10, k4, p16.
ROW 51: K16, p4, k10, p4, k10, p4, k16.

ROW 52: P16, **cable four back (c4b)** , p10, c4b, p10, c4b, p16.

To c4b, take the yarn back between the needles, slip the next two sts onto the cable needle and take it to the back.

Knit the next two sts on the left-hand needle. Bring the cable needle between the needles to the front and knit the two stitches on it.

This completes the c4b. Take the yarn between the needles to the front and continue.

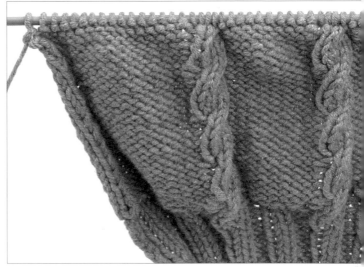

6-row patt repeat

ROW 1: K16, p4, k10, p4, k10, p4, k16.
ROW 2: P16, k4, p10, k4, p10, k4, p16.
ROW 3: K16, p4, k10, p4, k10, p4, k16.
ROW 4: P16, k4, p10, k4, p10, k4, p16.
ROW 5: K16, p4, k10, p4, k10, p4, k16.
ROW 6: P16, c4b, p10, c4b, p10, c4b, p16.

ROW 77. K16, p4, k10, p4, k10, p4, k16.
ROW 78: P16, k4, p10, k4, p10, k4, p16.
ROW 79: K16, p4, k10, p4, k10, p4, k16.
ROW 80: P16, k4, p10, k4, p10, k4, p16.

ROWS 53–76: Rep the 6-row patt repeat four times.

ROW 81: **Knit two stitches together (k2tog)**, k14, p4, k10, p4, k10, p4, k14, k2tog. *(62 sts)*

ROW 82: Purl two stitches together (p2tog) [20], p13, c4b, p10, c4b, p10, c4b, p13, p2tog.
(60 sts)

ROW 83: K2tog, k12, p4, k10, p4, k10, p4, k12, k2tog.
(58 sts)

ROW 84: P2tog, p11, k4, p10, k4, p10, k4, p11, p2tog.
(56 sts)

ROW 85: K2tog, [k2, k2tog, k2, k2tog, k2, p4] three times, [k2, k2tog] three times.
(46 sts)

ROW 86: P9, [k4, p8] twice, k4, p9.

ROW 87: K2tog, k1, k2tog, k1, k2tog, k1, [p4, k1, k2tog, k2, k2tog, k1] twice, p4, k1, k2tog, k1, k2tog, k1, k2tog.
(36 sts)

ROW 88: P6, [c4b, p6] three times.

ROW 89: K2tog, k1, k2tog, k1, [p4, k1, k2tog, k2tog, k1] twice, p4, k1, k2tog, k1, k2tog.
(28 sts)

ROW 90: P4, [k4, p4] three times.

ROW 91: K2tog, k2, [p4, k1, k2tog, k1] twice, p4, k2, k2tog.

(24 sts)

ROW 92: P3, [k4, p3] three times.

ROW 93: K2tog, k1, [p4, k3] twice, p4, k1, k2tog.

(22 sts)

ROW 94: P2, [c4b, p3] twice, c4b, p2.

ROW 95: K2tog, [p4, k3] twice, p4, k2tog.

(20 sts)

Bind (cast) off knitwise.

Handle

Make a slip knot 12 in. (30 cm) from the end of the yarn and, using the thumb cast-on method, cast on 12 sts.

ROW 1: Knit.

ROW 2: Purl.

Rep rows 1–2 until the work measures 12 in. (30 cm) long. Bind (cast) off.

Finishing

Weave in ends ⑥, including those on the handle. Gently **press** ⑬ the reverse stockinette (stocking) stitch edges.

RS facing and using **mattress stitch** ㉙, sew up 6½ in. (17 cm) of the rib on one side. The raw edges of the seam will be on the RS of the bag.

Turn the bag right-side out and bring the needle and yarn through to the RS. Keeping the mattress stitches even, sew up the rest of the rib so that the raw edges of this part of the seam are on the WS.

Cont sewing and sew the reverse stockinette (stocking) stitch sides together.

Sew across the bottom of the bag, matching the ends of the cables carefully. Then sew up the other side of the bag, reversing the stitching on the rib to match the first side.

Fold the handle in half lengthwise, stockinette (stocking) stitch-side out. Using mattress stitch, sew the long seam.

Turn the rib cuff over so that the bottom edge is level with the start of the rib section. Firmly stitch one end of the handle to the seam on each side of the inside of the bag. Pinch the sides of the handle in with a stitch for a neat finish and take two stitches through the rib to catch the back of the turned-over section and hold it in place.

The numbers in the squares refer to instructions in the Workshop sections.

83

Lacy shawl

This is the perfect project for novelty yarns and works best with needles two or three sizes larger than the spinner's recommended needle sizes. A fluffy yarn is harder to unpick if necessary, but it will conceal any occasional errors in the pattern.

Size

15 in. × 60 in. (38 cm × 1.5m)

You will need

Two 1¾oz (50g) balls of Rowan Kidsilk Haze in deep pink

US 10½ (7mm) needles
US 13 (9mm) needles
Tapestry needle

Gauge (tension) swatch

Make a **slip knot** 14 in. (35.5 cm) from the end of the yarn and, using US 10½ (7mm) and the **thumb cast-on method** *wait*, cast on 22 sts.

ROWS 1–8: Knit (k) .

ROW 9: K1, [knit two stitches together (k2tog) , **yarnover (yo)** 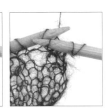, **purl (p)** 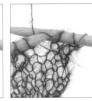 **1 st]** rep to last 3 sts, k2tog, yo, k1.

ROW 10 (WS): P3, [k1, p2] rep to last 4 sts, k1, p3.
As a check that the pattern (patt) is correct, the first purl stitch of the repeat is worked into the yarn over. If a yarnover has been missed, **make one (m1)** 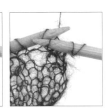 *to keep the patt correct.*

ROW 11: K1, yo, slip one, knit one, pass the slipped stitch over, (skpo) 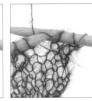, [p1, yo, skpo] rep to the last stitch, k1.

ROW 12 (WS): Rep row 10.
This time the second purl of the repeat is worked into the yarnover. If a yarnover has been missed, m1 to keep the patt correct.

Rep rows 9–12 seven times more, or until the patt can be knitted confidently.
Chanting the patt repeat as you knit is a sure way of keeping the patt correct, but noting what lies beneath the stitch as the patt is repeated is also a useful way of maintaining the patt.

Knit 8 rows.

Using a US 13 (9mm) needle in the right hand, **bind (cast) off** the stitches from the US 10½ (7mm) needle used to knit the swatch.

The numbers in the squares refer to instructions in the Workshop sections.

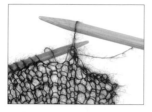

Pull the knitted loops through to a length of about ⅞ in. (2 cm).

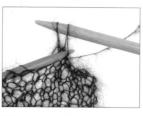

Without pulling tight, pass the loops over each other to bind (cast) off.

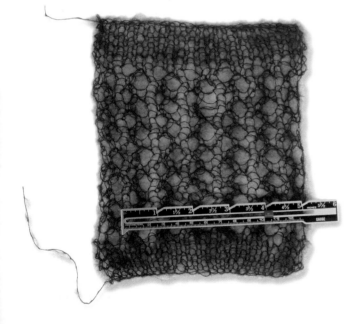

Measure the swatch 8 over the lace patt.
There should be 14 stitches and 26 rows to 4 in. (10 cm). In this case, the fit is not crucial so an approximate match will be sufficient.
However, note that a different gauge (tension) will affect the amount of yarn required. Remember to match the dye lot numbers on the ball bands if more yarn is required after the initial purchase.

Shawl

Make a slip knot 14 in. (35.5 cm) from the end of the yarn and, using US 10½ (7mm) needles and the thumb cast-on method, cast on 55 sts.

ROWS 1–8: Knit.

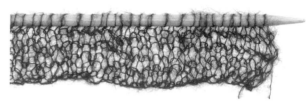

ROW 9: K1, [k2tog, yo, p1] rep to last 3 sts, k2tog, yo, k1.
ROW 10 (WS): P3, [k1, p2] rep to last 4 sts, k1, p3.
ROW 11: K1, yo, skpo, [p1, yo, skpo] rep to last st, k1.
ROW 12 (WS): Rep row 10.
Rows 9–12 form patt.
Check periodically that there are still 55 sts on the needle. The stitches are easier to count after a wrong-side row has been completed.

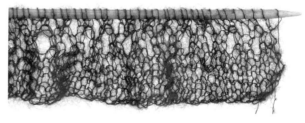

Cont in patt until the shawl measures 58 in. (147 cm) from the cast-on edge, or until at least 25 yds (23 m) of yarn remains on the ball.
In order to measure back from the end of a ball of yarn, continue working until about an eighth of the ball remains. Wind the remainder of yarn around a piece of card until the end is reached. Measure back from the end of the ball of yarn and make a slip knot. Starting from the yarn end, wind up the yarn into a ball. Continue to work the stitches until you come to the end of a WS row close to the slip knot.

End with a wrong side row.
Knit the next 8 rows.

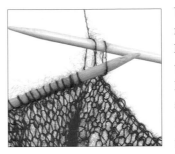

Using a US 13 (9mm) needle in the right hand, bind (cast off) the stitches very loosely, as for the swatch, from the US 10½ (7mm) needle used to knit the shawl.

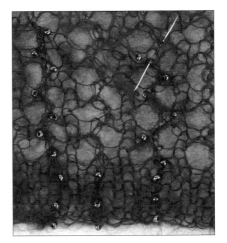

VARIATION

The shawl can be beaded to add weight and sparkle. Thread a length of yarn onto a needle that is fine enough to take a bead. Then, weave the thread up the zigzag patt, periodically attaching a bead. Alternatively, only add beads to the cast-on and bound (cast) off edge.

The numbers in the squares refer to instructions in the Workshop sections.

Kimono jacket

This very loose-fitting garment is a large project, but it is knitted in thick yarn on large needles and so it "grows" quickly. It is also very simple to work as it consists of only two pieces and has a minimum of shaping.

Size (one size)

chest	66 in. (168 cm)
neck to cuff	23½ in. (60 cm)
nape to hem	23½ in. (60 cm)

You will need

Ten 3½oz (100g) balls of Rowan Yorkshire Tweed Chunky in dark brown

US 11 (8mm) needles
US 10 (6mm) needles
Tapestry needle

Gauge (tension) swatch

Using US 11 (8mm) needles and the **cable cast-on method** 🔲, cast on 30 sts.

ROW 1: **Knit (k)** 🔳.

ROW 2: **Purl (p)** .

Rep rows 1–2 until 30 rows have been worked.

Bind (cast) off .

Measure the swatch 8.
Counting rows and stitches 18. There should be 11 stitches and 17 rows to 4 in. (10 cm).

Pattern repeats

These pattern repeats are indicated at various point in the pattern. Refer to the correct one below.

First 10-row patt repeat

ROW 1: Knit.
ROW 2: Purl.
Rep rows 1–2 three times more.
ROW 9: Knit.
ROW 10 (RIDGE ROW): Knit.

Second 10-row pattern repeat

ROW 1: Knit.
ROW 2: Purl to last 5 sts, k5.
Rep rows 1–2 three times more.
ROW 9: Knit.
ROW 10 (RIDGE ROW): Knit.

Third 10-row pattern repeat

ROW 1: Knit.
ROW 2: K5, purl to last 5 sts, k5.
Rep rows 1–2 three times more.
ROW 9: Knit.
ROW 10 (RIDGE ROW): Knit.

Construction diagram

The front and back of the jacket are knitted in exactly the same way—from cuff to cuff—but the back does not have an opening. This diagram will help you to establish where you are in the pattern as you knit.

Front

Make a **slip knot** ▉ approximately 30 in. (70 cm) from the end of the yarn. Using US 11 (8mm) needles and the **thumb cast-on method** ▉, cast on 30 sts.

Right cuff

ROW 1–5: Knit.

Right sleeve

Work the first 10-row patt repeat five times, ending on row 55.

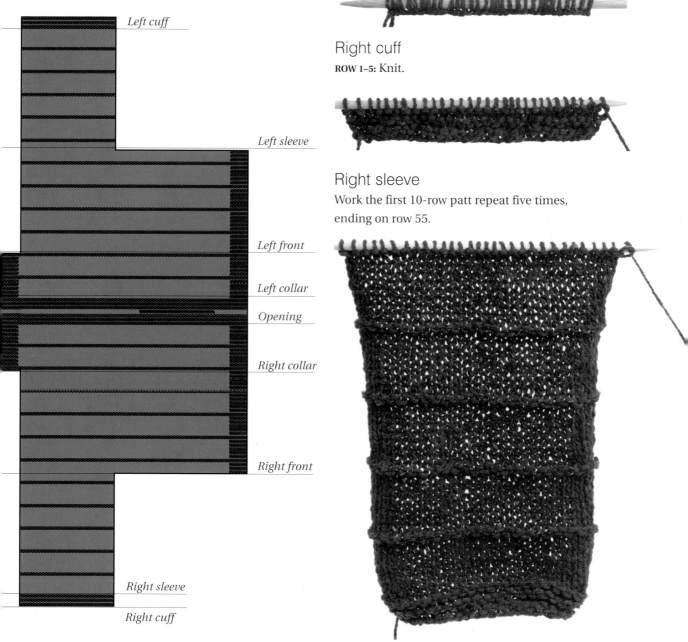

Left cuff

Left sleeve

Left front

Left collar

Opening

Right collar

Right front

Right sleeve

Right cuff

The numbers in the squares refer to instructions in the Workshop sections.

Right front

ROW 55 (WS): At the end of this row, using the cable cast-on method, cast on 36 stitches loosely. *(66 sts)*

Work the second 10-row patt repeat (page 90) four times, ending on row 95.

ROW 96: Knit.

ROW 97: Purl to last 5 sts, k5.

Rep rows 96–97 three times more.

Right collar

ROW 104: Knit to end, turn work, using the cable cast-on method, cast on 5 sts loosely. *(71 sts)*

ROW 105 (RIDGE ROW): Knit.

Work the third 10-row patt repeat (page 90) twice, ending on row 125.

Neck opening

ROWS 126–130: Knit.

ROW 131: Loosely bind (cast) off 36 sts knitwise, k19, loosely bind (cast)

off the remaining 15 sts knitwise. Break yarn. *(20 sts)*

Using the thumb cast-on method, loosely cast on 15 sts onto the empty needle.

ROW 132: With the needle holding the cast-on sts in the right hand, knit the 20 sts on the left-hand needle,

turn work and, using the cable cast-on method, cast on 36 sts loosely. *(71 sts)*

ROWS 133–135: Knit.

Left collar

Work the third 10-row patt repeat twice, ending on row 155.

ROW 156: Knit.

ROW 157: Loosely bind (cast) off 5 sts knitwise, purl to last 5 sts, k5.

Left front

ROW 158: Knit.

ROW 159: Purl to last 5 sts, k5.

Rep rows 158–159 twice more.

ROW 164: Knit.

ROW 165 (RIDGE ROW): Knit.

The numbers in the squares refer to instructions in the Workshop sections.

Work the second 10-row patt repeat three times, ending on row 195.

ROW 196: Knit.

ROW 197: Purl to last 5 sts, k5.
Rep row 196–197 three times more.

ROW 204: Knit.

ROW 205 (RIDGE ROW): K30, loosely bind (cast) off 36 sts purlwise.
(30 sts)

Left sleeve

Rejoin yarn.

Work the first 10-row patt repeat five times, ending on row 255.

Left cuff

ROWS 256–259: Knit.

Bind (cast) off loosely.

Back

Make a slip knot approximately 30 in. (70 cm) from the end of the yarn.
Using US 11 (8mm) needles and the thumb cast-on method, cast on 30 sts.

Left cuff

ROWS 1–5: Knit.

Left sleeve

Work the first 10-row patt repeat four times, then rep rows 1–9, ending on row 54.

Left back

ROW 55: Knit, at the end of this row using the cable cast-on method, cast on 36 stitches loosely.
(66 sts)
Work the second 10-row patt repeat four times, ending on row 95.
ROW 96: Knit.
ROW 97: Purl to last 5 sts, k5.
Rep rows 96–97 three times more.

Collar

ROW 104: Knit to end and, using the cable cast-on method, cast on 5 sts loosely.
(71 sts)
ROW 105 (RIDGE ROW): Knit.
Work the third 10-row patt repeat five times, ending on row 155.
ROW 156: Knit.

Right back

ROW 157: Loosely bind (cast) off 5 sts knitwise, purl to last 5 sts, k5.

ROW 158: Knit.

ROW 159: Purl to last 5 sts, k5.

Work rows 158–159 twice more.

ROW 164: Knit.

ROW 165 (RIDGE ROW): Knit.

Work the second 10-row patt repeat three times, ending on row 195.

ROW 196: Knit.

ROW 197: Purl to last 5 sts, k5.

Work row 196–197 three times more.

ROW 204: Knit.

ROW 205 (RIDGE ROW): K30, loosely bind (cast) off 36 sts purlwise.

(30 sts)

Right sleeve

Work the first 10-row patt repeat five times, ending on row 255.

Right cuff

ROWS 256–259: Knit.

Bind (cast) off loosely.

Ties (make 2)

Make a slip knot approximately 26 in. (65 cm) from the end of the yarn. Using US 10 (6mm) needles and the cable cast-on method, cast on 40 sts.

Bind (cast) off all sts.

Finishing

Weave in ends **G**, including those on the ties. **Block and press E** the front, back and ties.

WS facing and using **mattress stitch 29**, sew the front and back together. Sew from collar to cuff and from cuff to hem on each side.

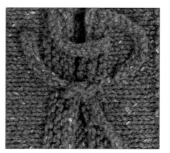

Thread the ties through the garter stitch edging either side of the opening.

The numbers in the squares refer to instructions in the Workshop sections.

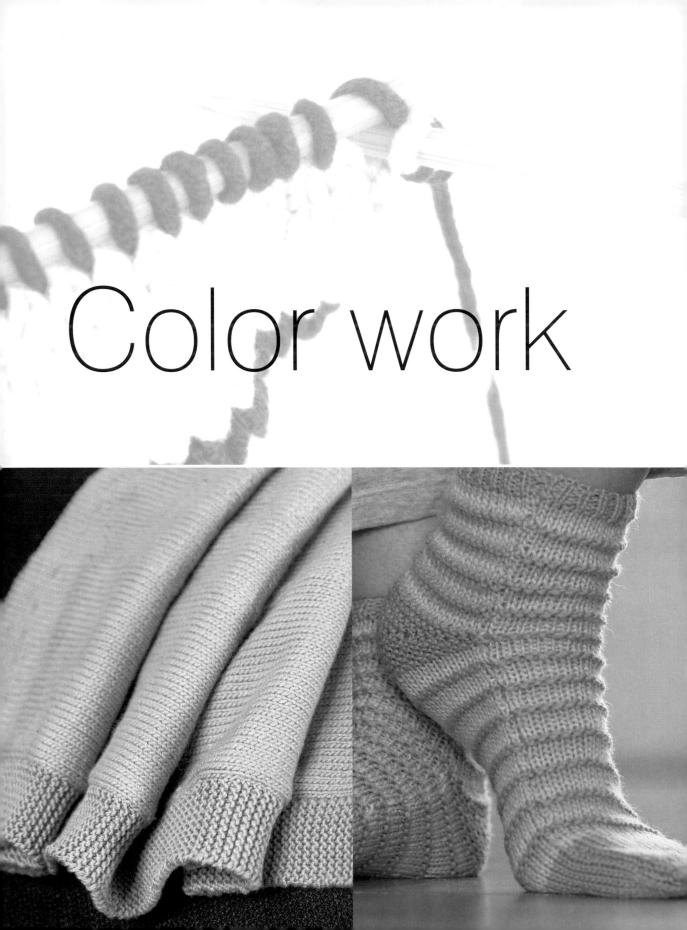

Color work

Workshop

Color knitting is something that beginners often shy away from, and indeed some more experienced knitters avoid. However, it really isn't that difficult to do and it does add enormously to your knitting repertoire. Three color knitting techniques—stripes, intarsia and Fair Isle—are covered in this chapter, all with simple projects specially designed to get you started on color work.

You will need

Any durable yarn can be used. Check the manufacturer's band for information on the suggested needle sizes and if a range is suggested, chose the middle size.
The yarn and needles used for the practice swatches in this book are:

Rowan All Seasons Cotton 1¾oz (50g)

1 pair US 7 (4.5mm) needles

Gauge (tension)

The gauge (tension) does not matter too much at this stage; just concentrate on achieving a comfortable flow that will keep the stitches even.

30 Stripes

Stripes are a quick and easy way to add color to a knitting project.

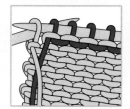

To change yarn colors, pass the working yarn under the yarn not in use before knitting the last stitch in the row.

To practice this stitch

Use two contrasting yarns.
Cast on 15 sts using the **cable cast-on method 15**.
ROW 1: **Knit (k) 3** in A.
ROW 2: **Purl (p) 16** in A.
Rep rows 1–2 once more.
ROW 5: Knit in B.
ROW 6: Purl in B until the last stitch, secure yarn A and purl the last stitch in B.
Rep rows 5–6 once more.
ROW 9: Knit A.
ROW 10: Purl A until the last stitch, secure yarn B and purl the last stitch in A.
Rep rows 9–10 once more.
Rep rows 5–12 once more.
Bind (cast) off 19.

The numbers in the squares refer to instructions in the Workshop sections.

97

31 Intarsia

Intarsia is a technique of color knitting used when the color forms blocks within a design. The word *intarsia* describes the method of securing the blocks of color together. It forms a single layer fabric, which means it is economical with yarn and has a drape similar to single color fabric.

To change the colors, knit the last stitch in the old color yarn, insert the right needle into the next stitch, and pass the new yarn under the old before working the knit stitch. The technique is exactly the same on a purl row.

Weave in ends

Weave in the ends through the side stitches of the block of the same color, first going clockwise around the shape and then back again in the opposite direction.

Reading a chart

Color work is often illustrated with a chart as this has the advantage of giving a pictorial idea of what the pattern should look like and making it easy to identify where you are in a sequence. Each block or square on the chart represents one stitch and is coded to represent a stitch color, or sometimes a stitch technique, but these may differ from pattern to pattern so check the key carefully.

The chart represents the design from the right side, so all the odd-numbered rows are read from right to left, just as you would knit the stitches across the left-hand needle. All the even-numbered rows are read from left to right, as the stitches are worked across the back of the work. Take your time and

check that the first few rows are correct, and then proceed with confidence, working out the new stitch positions by their relationship to those already worked. A chart doesn't always show the whole project stitch-by-stitch but perhaps a repeating sequence of stitches or a small motif, in which case an instruction will be given for its position.

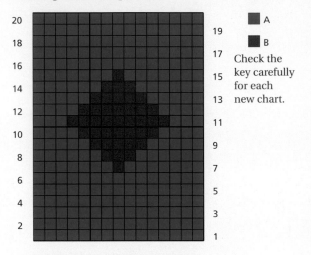

■ A

■ B

Check the key carefully for each new chart.

To practice this technique

Use two contrasting yarns.

Cast on 15 sts using the **cable cast-on method 15** .

ROWS 1–6: Work the chart above in **stockinette (stocking) stitch (St st) 17** .

ROW 7: K7, join the second color and continue using the **intarsia** technique.

Bind (cast) off 19 .

32 Stranding

Stranding is a technique used to create traditional Fair Isle designs and is suitable for patterns where a yarn is used across the row with not more than three or four stitches of another color between. The loops of yarn (the floats) on the wrong side make the knitted fabric both dense and warm.

On a knit row

1 Knit the last stitch in the old color yarn.

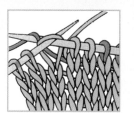

2 Pick up the new color yarn by reaching under the old one. Knit the next stitch in the new color.

On a purl row

1 Purl the last stitch in the old color. Purl the next stitch in the new color.

2 The float at the back of the work should have a slight droop from the horizontal to retain some of the elasticity of the knitting.

To practice this technique

Use two contrasting yarns.

Cast on 15 sts using the background color and the **cable cast-on method 15**.

ROWS 1–8: Work the chart below in **stockinette (stocking) stitch (St st) 17**.

ROW 9: K2, join the second color and use stranding to continue following the chart.

Bind (cast) off 19.

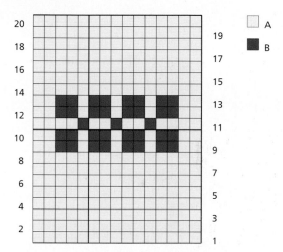

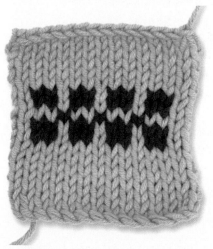

The numbers in the squares refer to instructions in the Workshop sections.

99

Beach bag

This project is knitted in a very simple stripe pattern that looks good when it is a bag, but also looks attractive when the bag is unbuttoned to become a beach mat.

Size

As a bag: 15¾ x 19½ in. (40 x 50 cm)

As a mat: 31½ x 19½ in. (80 x 50 cm)

You will need

3½oz (100g) balls of Rowan All Seasons Cotton

Two in red (A)

Three in lime green (B)

Three in blue (C)

Twelve ½ in. (12mm) buttons in red

US 7 (4.5mm) needles

Tapestry needle

Gauge (tension) swatch

Make a **slip knot** 18 in. (45 cm) from the end of yarn A and, using the **thumb cast-on method** , cast on 25 sts.

ROW 1: [**Knit (k)** **purl (p)** 🔢 1 st,] rep to the last
🔢 1 st, stitch, k1.

Rep row 1 four times to make **seed (moss) stitch** 🔢 edge.

ROW 6: [K1, p1] rep to last 2 sts, join in yarn B, but p1, k1 in yarn A.

ROW 7: Knit in yarn B.

ROW 8: Using yarn B purl to last 2 sts, carry yarn A by looping yarn B under it, purl to the end of the row using yarn B.

ROW 9: Using yarn B knit to last 2 sts, join in yarn C, knit the end of the row in yarn B.

ROW 10: Using yarn C, P1, carry yarn B by looping yarn C under it before purling the next stitch. Purl to last 2 sts, carry yarn A by looping yarn C under it, purl to the end of the row using yarn C.

ROW 11: Knit in yarn C.

ROW 12: Using yarn C, p1, carry yarn B by looping yarn C under it, purl the next stitch. Purl to last 2 sts, carry yarn A by looping yarn C under it, purl to the end of the row using yarn C.

ROW 13: Knit in yarn A.

The **stripes** 30 color sequence conts as folls:
3 rows yarn B,
3 rows yarn C and
1 row yarn A.
On each purl row, secure the yarn hanging at the beginning and end of the row.
Cont until 5 yarn C stripes have been completed.
Using yarn A **bind (cast) off** 19.

The numbers in the squares refer to instructions in the Workshop sections.

101

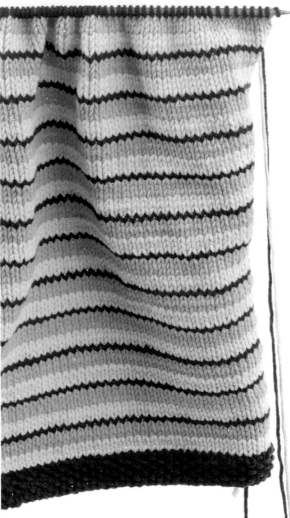

Measure the swatch 🖪.

Counting rows and stitches 🔞. There should be 18 stitches and 25 rows to 4 in. (10 cm).

Bag

Make a slip knot 48 in. (122 cm) from the end of yarn A and, using the thumb cast-on method, cast on 75 sts.

ROW 1: [K1, p1] rep to last st, k1.

This creates the seed (moss) stitch edging.

Cont as for swatch, with 4 rows more of seed (moss) stitch and joining in yarn B.

The stripe sequence is also the same as worked for the swatch.

Cont until 12 yarn A (red) stripes, excluding the edging, have been worked. The last yarn A (red) stripe is a purl row.

This is the fold of the bag, or the center of the mat, and beyond this the stripe sequence is reversed.

Cut C, B, and A yarns 4 in. (10 cm) from the last stitch worked.

ROWS 91-93: Join in yarn C (blue) and work in **stockinette (stocking) stitch (St st)** 🔳.

ROWS 94-96: Join in the yarn B and work in St st.

ROW 97: Join in yarn A and knit.

✳ **ROWS 98-100:** Using yarn C work in St st.
ROWS 101-102: Using yarn B work in St st.

ROW 103 BUTTONHOLE ROW: Using yarn B k2, bind (cast) off 3 sts,

*For a neat **buttonhole** 27, knit the stitches firmly before binding (casting) them off.*

work to the last 5 sts, bind (cast) off 3 sts, k1.

ROW 104 BUTTONHOLE COMPLETED ROW: Using yarn A P1, carry yarn B by looping yarn A under it, p1, cast on 3 sts.

Purl to the next set of bound (cast) off stitches and cast on 3 sts, as before. Carry yarn C by looping yarn A under it and p2 using yarn A.✳

With the yarn now joined in, rep from ✳ to ✳ until 12 buttonholes have been made and completed, six on each side.
Using yarn A (red) only.
ROW 175: [K1, p1] rep to last st, k1.
Rep row 175 four times more.
Bind (cast) off in the seed (moss) stitch patt set.

Straps (make 2)

Make a slip knot 6 in. (15 cm) from the end of yarn A and, using the thumb cast-on method, cast on 11 sts.
ROWS 1–6: [K1, p1] rep to last stitch, k1.

ROW 7: Join yarn B and knit.
ROW 8: Join yarn C and purl.
ROW 9: Knit row in yarn A.

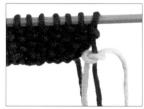

The stripe patt is worked in St st in the foll color sequence, one row in each color: B, C, A.
There is no need to carry the unused yarn on the wrong side because the stripe sequence is only 3 rows long.

The numbers in the squares refer to instructions in the Workshop sections.

Cont until the strap measures about 30 in. (76 cm) long and the last row is a purl row worked in yarn C.

NEXT ROW: Using yarn A, [k1, p1], rep to the last stitch, k1.
Rep the last row five times more.

Bind (cast) off in seed (moss) stitch patt set.

Finishing

Block and press 🔢 the bag and strap carefully.
Weave in ends 🔢.

Fold the strap in half, St st inward, leaving the ends of the yarn hanging loose.
Mattress stitch 🔢 the long edges together, starting with the first lower yarn B (lime green) ridge loop on the left.

Cont up the seam, selecting the lower row ridge loops on the left and the upper row ridge loops on the right in the foll color sequence: A, C, B (red, blue, lime green). Weave the ends into the center of the strap.

Unbuttoned, this bag makes an ideal beach mat.

Sew the strap to the inside of the bag about 4 in. (10 cm) in from the edge.

Fold the bag in half and sew on the buttons so that they correspond with the buttonholes.

Socks

These socks are an excellent addition to any knitter's repertoire. They are worked on two needles with a seam at the side and are perfect for a range of colorful designs. Look at them again when you have had more practice and exchange the stripes for motifs.

Size

Adult medium. The foot length can be varied.

You will need

3½oz (100g) balls of Jaeger Matchmaker Merino DK
    One in lilac (A)
    One in pink (B)
    One in blue (C)

US 5 (3.75 mm) needles
US 6 (4 mm) needles
Tapestry needle

Gauge (tension) swatch

Make a **slip knot** ❶ 18 in. (45 cm) from the end of yarn A and, using **thumb cast-on method** ❷ and US 6 (4mm) needles, cast on 30 sts.

Work 4 rows in **stockinette (stocking) stitch (St st)** ⓱.

At the beginning of the next row, join in yarn B by inserting the right-hand needle into the first stitch and looping the yarn over the needle. Pull the loop through to form the stitch.

The numbers in the squares refer to instructions in the Workshop sections.

105

Knit along the rest of the row with yarn B and work the foll row in St st.

At the beginning of the next row, join in yarn C as for yarn B.

Work two rows in St st and yarn C. There should be three yarn colors hanging off the right-hand side of the swatch. Gently pull each strand to ease the last stitch knitted to match the gauge (tension) of the rest of the swatch.

Pattern repeat

ROW 9: Insert the right needle into the first stitch. Select yarn A from under yarn B and C and knit the row in yarn A.

ROW 10: Knit in yarn A.

ROW 11: Insert the right needle into the first stitch. Select yarn B from under yarn A and C and knit the row in yarn B.

ROW 12: Purl in yarn B.

ROW 13: Insert the right needle into the first stitch. Select yarn C from under yarn A and B and knit the row in yarn C.
ROW 14: Purl in yarn C.
Rep the **stripes** 🔟 pattern (patt) four times more.

ROW 39: Knit in yarn A.
ROW 40: Purl in yarn A.
ROW 41: Knit in yarn B.
ROW 42: Purl in yarn B.
ROW 43: Knit in yarn C.
ROW 44: Purl in yarn C.
ROW 45: Knit in yarn A.
ROW 46: Purl in yarn A.
ROW 47: Knit in yarn A.
ROW 48: Purl in yarn A.

Bind (cast) off 🔟.

Measure the swatch 🔟.
Counting rows and stitches 🔟. There should be 22 stitches and 28 rows to 4 in. (10 cm).

The back of the right-hand edge of the swatch should have no long loops of unused yarn. Ease the end stitches tight as you knit.

Right sock
Cuff

Make a slip knot 22 in. (65 cm) from the end of yarn A and, using the thumb cast-on method, and US 5 (3.75mm) needles, cast on 51 sts.

Rib is used to give a firm fit around the ankle.
ROW 1: [K1, p1] rep to last stitch, k1.
ROW 2: [P1, k1] rep to last stitch, p1.
Rep rows 1–2 twice more.

Now that the **rib 2** has been completed, change the needles to US 6 (4mm) needles by knitting row 7 with the new needle in the right hand and a US 5 (3.75mm) needle in the left and then purling row 8 with two US 6 (4mm) needles.

ROW 7: Join in yarn B, k25, **knit two stitches together (k2tog) 1**, k24 using yarn B.
(50 sts)
ROW 8: Purl in yarn B.

ROW 9: Join in yarn C and knit to the end of the row using yarn C.
ROW 10: Purl in yarn C.

Cont for another 36 rows using the patt repeat from the gauge (tension) swatch.

Heel

A sock is basically a tube with a right-angle bend. Knitting some stitches more often than others can create a right-angle bend but this creates small holes. Knitting the heel in garter stitch reduces these small holes.

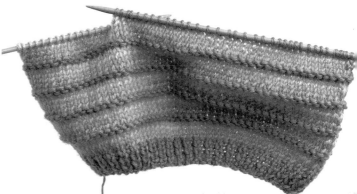

ROW 47 (RS): Using yarn A, k34, turn the work around, ready to knit back along the stitches just knitted.

ROW 48 (WS): K32, turn the work around.

ROW 49 (RS): K30, turn the work around.
ROW 50 (WS): K28, turn the work around.
ROW 51 (RS): K26, turn the work around.
ROW 52 (WS): K24, turn the work around.
ROW 53 (RS): K22, turn the work around.
ROW 54 (WS): K20, turn the work around.
ROW 55 (RS): K18, turn the work around.
ROW 56 (WS): K16, turn the work around.
ROW 57 (RS): K14, turn the work around.

ROW 58 (WS): K12, turn the work around.

ROW 59 (RS): K10, turn the work around.

ROW 60 (WS): K8, turn the work around.

ROW 61 (RS): K6, turn the work around.

ROW 62 (WS): K4, turn the work around.

ROW 78 (WS): K46, k2tog, k1.
(48 sts)

Foot

Starting with a knit row and yarn B, continue to work in the patt repeat used in the gauge (tension) swatch. Continue until the foot measures the same distance as that from the heel to the top of the small toe of the recipient of the sock.

End with the second row of a yarn C (blue) stripe.

ROW 63 (RS): K5, turn the work around.

ROW 64 (WS): K6, turn the work around.

ROW 65 (RS): K8, turn the work around.

ROW 66 (WS): K10, turn the work around.

ROW 67 (RS): K12, turn the work around.

ROW 68 (WS): K14, turn the work around.

ROW 69 (RS): K16, turn the work around.

ROW 70 (WS): K18, turn the work around.

ROW 71 (RS): K20, turn the work around.

ROW 72 (WS): K22, turn the work around.

ROW 73 (RS): K24, turn the work around.

ROW 74 (WS): K26, turn the work around.

ROW 75 (RS): K28, turn the work around.

ROW 76 (WS): K30, turn the work around.

ROW 77 (RS): K30, k2tog, knit to end of row.

Toe

The sock will now be tapered to shape around the toes. Using yarn A, work 2 rows in St st.

Decreases are made in the same position in the center of the row, so the number of stitches before a decrease goes down by 1 st with each row.

ROW 1: K21, **slip one, knit one, pass the slipped stitch over (skpo)** ⬚, k2, k2tog, k21.
(46 sts)

ROW 2: For this row and each even-numbered row, purl.

ROW 3: K20, skpo, k2, k2tog, k20.

(44 sts)

ROW 5: K19, skpo, k2, k2tog, k19.

(42 sts)

ROW 7: K18, skpo, k2, k2tog, k18.

(40 sts)

ROW 9: K17, skpo, k2, k2tog, k17.

(38 sts)

ROW 11: K16, skpo, k2, k2tog, k16.

(36 sts)

ROW 13: K15, skpo, k2, k2tog, k15.

(34 sts)

Decreases are now also made at both edges.

ROW 15: K2, skpo, k10, skpo, k2, k2tog, k10, k2tog, k2.

(30 sts)

ROW 17: K2, skpo, k8, skpo, k2, k2tog, k8, k2tog, k2.

(26 sts)

ROW 19: K2, skpo, k6, skpo, k2, k2tog, k6, k2tog, k2.

(22 sts)

ROW 20: Purl.

Bind (cast) off.

Left sock
Cuff

Cast on and work as for the right sock.

(50 sts)

Heel

ROW 47 (RS): K48, turn the work around.

Continue to follow the patt for the right sock until row 77 has been completed.

ROW 78 (WS): K32, k2tog, knit to the end of the row.

(48 sts)

Foot and toe

Foll the patt instructions for the right sock.

Finishing

Weave in ends **G**. Thread a length of yarn onto a tapestry needle and sew the seam using **mattress stitch 29**. Start at the cuff matching the stripes on either edge carefully.

To reduce the bulk of the seam, turn the sock inside out, lightly spray with water or a jet of steam and press and roll out the seam with the fingers until it is dry and set.

The numbers in the squares refer to instructions in the Workshop sections.

Striped throw

This design uses simple two-color intarsia knitting to achieve a surprisingly complex effect.
You can make a larger throw if you wish by simply knitting more strips.

Size

40 × 31 in. (102 × 79 cm)

You will need

Five 1¾oz (50g) balls of Rowan Wool Cotton
in mauve (A)

Five 1¾oz (50g) balls of Rowan Wool Cotton
in lilac (B)

US 3 (3.25mm) needles
Tapestry needle

Gauge (tension) swatch

Using the **cable cast-on
method** 🔢 and yarn A, cast
on 30 sts.

ROW 1: Knit (k) 🔢.

ROW 2: Purl (p) 🔢.
These 2 rows form the
**stockinette (stocking)
stitch** 🔢 **(St st) patt.**
Rep rows 1–2 until 40
rows have been worked.
Bind (cast) off 🔢.

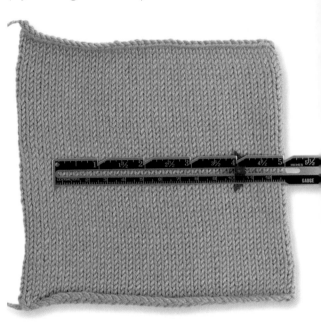

Measure the swatch 🔢.
Counting rows and stitches 🔢. There should be
26 stitches and 37 rows to 4 in (10 cm).

Making the throw
Diamond strips (make four)

Using the cable cast-on method and yarn A, cast on
32 sts.
ROW 1: Knit.
ROW 2: Purl.

Rep rows 1–2 once more, then rep row 1 once more.

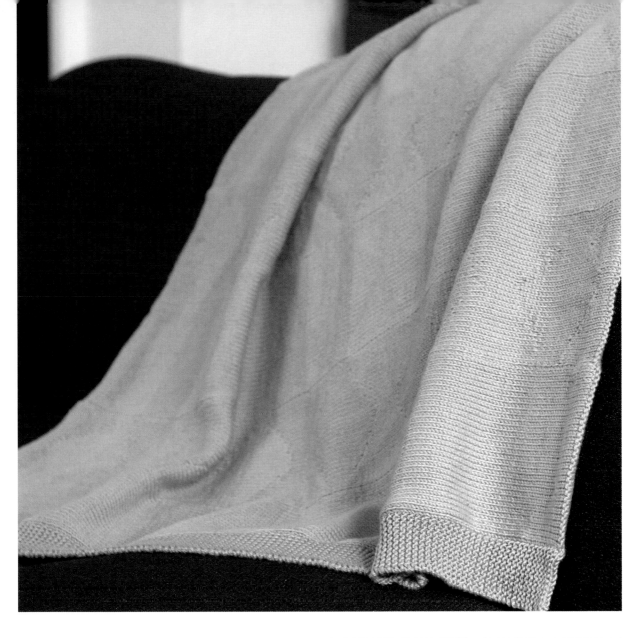

ROW 6 (FOLD ROW): Knit.

ROW 1 (OF PATT REPEAT): Knit in A.

ROW 2: Purl in A.

Rep rows 1–2 once more.

ROW 5: Knit in A.

ROW 6: P15 in A, put the needle through the next st, loop yarn B over the needle and p2 in B,

carry yarn A loosely across the back of the 2 sts and p15 in A.

The numbers in the squares refer to instructions in the Workshop sections.

ROW 7: K14 in A, put the needle through the next st, pick up yarn B, take it over yarn A and around the needle and k4 in B,

put the needle through the next st, loop the end of a new ball of yarn A over the needle and k14 in A.

ROW 8: P13 in A, put the needle through the next st, loop yarn B under yarn A and over the needle and p6 in B,

put the needle through the next st, loop yarn A over yarn B and p13 in A.

ROW 9: K12 in A, put the needle through the next st, pick up yarn B, take it over yarn A and around the needle and k8 in B,

put the needle through the next st, take yarn A over yarn B and over the needle and k12 in A.

Work rows 10–16 as instructed, referring to row 8 or 9 as needed for help with the **intarsia** 🔳 color change.
ROW 10: P11A, p10B, p11A.
ROW 11: K10A, k12B, k10A.
ROW 12: P9A, p14B, p9A.
ROW 13: K8A, k16B, k8A.

ROW 14: P7A, p18B, p7A.
ROW 15: K6A, k20B, k6A.

ROW 16: P5A, p22B, p5A, stranding yarn B along the WS of the last 5 sts.

ROW 17: Using the stranded yarn, knit in B.
ROW 18: Purl in B.

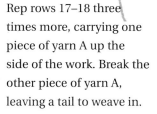

Rep rows 17–18 three times more, carrying one piece of yarn A up the side of the work. Break the other piece of yarn A, leaving a tail to weave in.

ROW 25: Using the piece of yarn A that was carried up the side, k5 in A, stranding yarn A along the WS of the 5 sts,

put the needle through the next st, loop yarn B under yarn A and around the needle and k22 in B, put the needle through the next st, loop the end of a new ball of yarn A over the needle and k5 in A.

ROW 26: P6 in A, put the needle through the next st, take yarn B under yarn A and around the needle and p20 in B,

put the needle through the next st, take yarn A under yarn B and around the needle and p6 in A.

Work rows 27–35 as instructed, referring to row 25 or 26 as needed for help with the color change.

ROW 27: K7A, k18B, k7A.

ROW 28: P8A, p16B, p8A.

ROW 29: K9A, k14B, k9A.

ROW 30: P10A, p12B, p10A.

ROW 31: K11A, k10B, k11A.

ROW 32: P12A, p8B, p12A.

ROW 33: K13A, k6B, k13A.

ROW 34: P14A, p4B, p14A.

ROW 35: K15A, k2B, k15A

ROW 36: Purl in A.

ROW 37: Knit in A. Rep rows 36–37 once more.

ROW 40: Purl in A.

The WS of the work should look like this.

Rep the 40-row diamond patt on page 114 six times more in the following sequence and using chart 1 for reference:

1ST REPEAT: Use yarn B instead of yarn A and yarn A instead of yarn B.

2ND REPEAT: As patt repeat given.

3RD–6TH REPEATS: As 1st repeat.

ROW 281 (FOLD ROW): Purl.

ROW 282: Knit.

Rep rows 281–282 twice more.

Bind (cast) off loosely purlwise.

Striped strips (make five)

Using the cable method and yarn A, cast on 32 sts.

ROW 1: Knit.

ROW 2: Purl.

Rep rows 1–2 once more, then rep row 1 once more.

ROW 6 (FOLD ROW): Knit.

ROW 1 (OF PATT REPEAT): Knit in A.

ROW 2: Purl in A.

Rep rows 1–2 seven times more.

ROW 17: Join yarn B. Rep rows 1–2 four times in yarn B,

carrying yarn A up the side of the rows.

The numbers in the squares refer to instructions in the Workshop sections.

ROW 25: Break off yarn B. Using yarn A, rep rows 1–2 eight times, finishing on row 40.

Rep the 40-row stripe patt on page 115 six times more in the following sequence and using chart 2 for reference:

1ST REPEAT: Use yarn B instead of yarn A and yarn A instead of yarn B.

2ND REPEAT: As patt repeat given.

3RD–6TH REPEATS: As 1st repeat.

ROW 281 (FOLD ROW): Purl.

ROW 282: Knit.

Rep rows 281–282 twice more.

Bind (cast) off loosely purlwise.

Finishing

Weave in ends 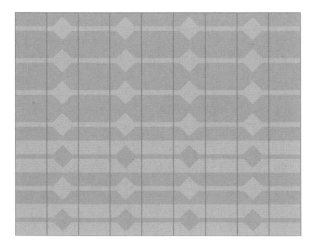 carefully to close holes.

Block and press strips.

Lay strips side by side following the diagram below.

40-row diamond patt repeat

ROW 1: Knit in A.	**ROW 25:** K5A, k22B, k5A.
ROW 2: Purl in A.	**ROW 26:** P6A, p20B, p6A.
Rep rows 1–2 once more.	**ROW 27:** K7A, k18B, k7A.
ROW 5: Knit in A.	**ROW 28:** P8A, p16B, p8A.
ROW 6: P15A, p2B, p15A.	**ROW 29:** K9A, k14B, k9A.
ROW 7: K14A, k4B, k14A.	**ROW 30:** P10A, p12B, p10A.
ROW 8: P13A, p6B, p13A.	**ROW 31:** K11A, k10B, k11A.
ROW 9: K12A, k8B, k12A.	**ROW 32:** P12A, p8B, p12A.
ROW 10: P11A, p10B, p11A.	**ROW 33:** K13A, k6B, k13A.
ROW 11: K10A, k12B, k10A.	**ROW 34:** P14A, p4B, p14A.
ROW 12: P9A, p14B, p9A.	**ROW 35:** K15A, k2B, k15A.
ROW 13: K8A, k16B, k8A.	**ROW 36:** Purl in A.
ROW 14: P7A, p18B, p7A.	**ROW 37:** Knit in A.
ROW 15: K6A, k20B, k6A.	Rep rows 36–37 once
ROW 16: P5A, p22B, p5A.	more.
ROW 17: Knit in B.	**ROW 40:** Purl in A.
ROW 18: Purl in B.	
Rep rows 17–18 three	
times more.	

A   B

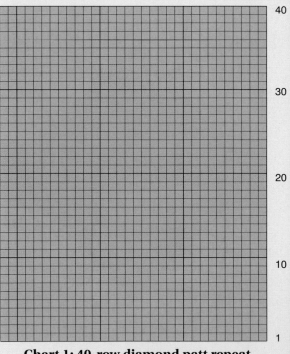

Chart 1: 40-row diamond patt repeat

40-row stripe patt repeat

ROW 1: Knit in A.

ROW 2: Purl in A.

Rep rows 1–2 seven times more.

ROW 17: Join in yarn B. Rep rows 1–2 four times in yarn B, carrying yarn A up the side of the rows.

ROW 25: Break off yarn B. Using yarn A, rep rows 1–2 eight times, finishing on row 40.

☐ A   ☐ B

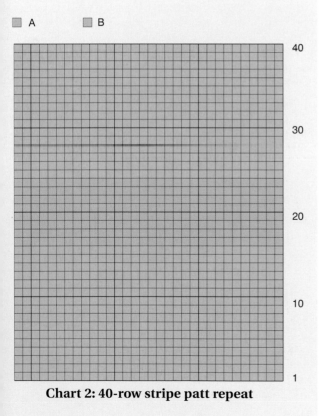

Chart 2: 40-row stripe patt repeat

The numbers in the squares refer to instructions in the Workshop sections.

Using **mattress stitch 29**, sew the strips together, matching the stripes and fold lines accurately.

Fold the top and bottom edges to the WS along the fold rows and slip stitch the hems in place.

Border (make 2)

Make a **slip knot 1** 10 in. (24 cm) from the end of the yarn A and, using the **thumb cast-on method 2**, cast on 12 sts.

ROW 1: Knit.

ROW 2: Knit.

Rep rows 1–2 until when slightly stretched the border fits along a side of the throw that is not hemmed.

Bind (cast) off.

Using mattress stitch, sew the borders to the sides of the throw that are not hemmed.

Baby jacket

This project is a simple introduction to Fair Isle knitting, so experiment with your own color combinations. Use any yarn left over to knit a pair of the bootees on page 20 to match.

Size

For a six-month-old child

Chest: 18 in. (46 cm)

Knitted measurements

Chest: 22 in. (56 cm)

Length: 10 in. (25 cm)

Sleeve: 9 in. (23 cm)

You will need

3½oz (100g) balls of Rowan Wool Cotton

    Three in beige (A)

    One in dark green (B)

    One in yellow (C)

    One in blue (D)

Five ¼ in. (6mm) pearl buttons

US 4 (3.5mm) needles

US 6 (4mm) needles

Tapestry needle

Safety pins

Gauge (tension) swatch

Make a **slip knot 1** 24 in. (60 cm) from the end of yarn A (beige) and using the **thumb cast-on method 2** and US 6 (4mm) needles, cast on 41 sts.

ROW 1: Purl (p) 16 1 st, **knit (k) 3** 1 st, p1, k1, p1, to create a **seed (moss) stitch 22** band at the edge. Knit to last 5 sts, p1, k1, p1, k1, p1 to create a seed (moss) stitch band on the other edge.

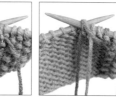

ROW 10: P1, k1, p1, k1, purl to last 4 sts, k1, p1, k1, p1. These two rows form the repeat for a **stockinette (stocking) stitch (St st) 17** pattern (patt) with a 5-st seed (moss) stitch band on each edge. Rep these two rows for a total of 21 rows; the last row is a knit row.

Cut a length of yarn B (dark green) 30 in. (76 cm) long.

ROW 22: P1, k1, p1, k1, p1, [p1B,   p2A],   Rep nine times more, p1B, then p1, k1, p1, k1, p1 in A.

This technique is described in **stranding 32**.

Push the stitches along the right-hand needle as they are worked. This helps to prevent the strands being pulled too tightly between color changes. At the end of the row, stretch the stitches along the needle and ease the stitches and strands so that all the stitches lie flat and the knitting is not puckered.

The numbers in the squares refer to instructions in the Workshop sections.

Unless otherwise stated, all the stitches are worked in beige (A).

Cut a length of yarn C (yellow) 37 in. (94 cm) long and rep the process.

ROW 23: P1, k1, p1, k1, p1, [k1, k2C] rep nine times more, k1, p1, k1, p1, k1, p1.

ROW 24: P1, k1, p1, k1, p1, [p1, p2C] rep nine times more, p2, k1, p1, k1, p1.

Cut a length of yarn D (blue) 30 in. (76 cm) long and rep the process.

ROW 25: P1, k1, p1, k1, p1, [k1D, k2] rep nine times more, k1D, then p1, k1, p1, k1, p1.

Cut a length of yarn C (yellow) 37 in. (94 cm) long and rep the process.

ROW 26: P1, k1, p1, k1, p1, [p1, p2C] rep nine times more, p2, k1, p1, k1, p1.

ROW 27: P1, k1, p1, k1, p1, [k1, k2C] rep nine times more, k1, p1, k1, p1, k1, p1.

Cut a length of yarn B (dark green) 37 in. (94 cm) long and rep the process.

ROW 28: P1, k1, p1, k1, p1, [p1B, p2] rep nine times more, p1B, p1, k1, p1, k1, p1.

Rep rows 1–2 for 22 rows.

Bind (cast) off ⓲.

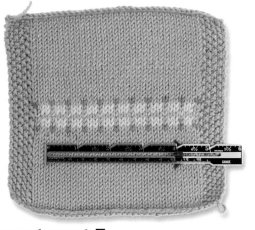

Measure the swatch ⓼.

Counting rows and stitches ⓲. There should be 24 stitches and 32 rows to 4 in. (10 cm).

Jacket

The front and back of the jacket are knitted in one piece to avoid bulky seams.

Make a slip knot 60 in. (1.5 m) from the end of the yarn and, using the thumb cast-on method, US 6 (4mm) needles and yarn A (beige) cast on 137 sts.

ROW 1: [P1, k1] rep to last st, p1.

Rep row 1 for 8 rows to create the seed (moss) stitch patt.

The seed (moss) stitch is worked on the first 5 and last 5 sts of each row to form the front facings at either end of every row. The remaining stitches are worked in St st with color work and increases and decreases as required to create the body.

ROW 9: P1, k1, p1, k1, p1, knit to last 5 sts, p1, k1, p1, k1, p1.

ROW 10: P1, k1, p1, k1, purl to last 4 sts, k1, p1, k1, p1.

Rep rows 9–10 once more.

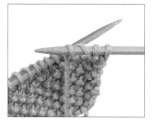

ROW 13 (BUTTONHOLE ROW): P1, k1, firmly **yarnover (yo)** ⓶ the needle twice,

knit two stitches together (k2tog) ⓫, p1, knit to last 5 sts, p1, k1, p1, k1, p1.

ROW 14 (COMPLETE BUTTON-HOLE ROW): P1, k1, p1, k1, purl to last 4 sts, drop the first loop of the double yarnover off the left-hand needle,

purl into the extra large yarnover loop created, k1, p1.

ROW 15: P1, k1, p1, k1, p1, knit to last 5 sts, p1, k1, p1, k1, p1.

ROW 16: P1, k1, p1, k1, purl to last 4 sts, k1, p1, k1, p1.

ROW 17: P1, k1, p1, k1, p1, knit to last 5 sts, p1, k1, p1, k1, p1.

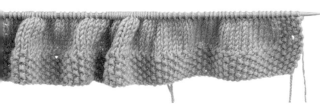

The color work starts on the next row. The patt is exactly the same as the swatch.

If working from the chart, in this case start from the bottom left because the first row is a purl row. Read the even-numbered rows from left to right for WS of work and read the odd-numbered rows from right to left for RS of work.

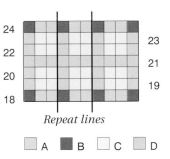

Repeat lines

☐ A ◼ B ☐ C ☐ D

The repeat lines on the chart represent the brackets in the patt copy.

Unless otherwise stated, all the stitches are worked in yarn A (beige).

ROW 18: P1, k1, p1, k1, p1, join in yarn B (dark green), [p1B, p2] rep 41 times more, p1B, p1, k1, p1, k1, p1. Cut the yarn B (dark green) 4 in. (10 cm) from the last stitch.

ROW 19: P1, k1, p1, k1, p1, k1, join in yarn C (yellow), [k2C, k1] rep 41 times more, p1, k1, p1, k1, p1.

ROW 20: P1, k1, p1, k1, p1, [p1, p2C] rep 41 times more, p2, k1, p1, k1, p1. Cut yarn C (yellow) 4 in. (10 cm) from the last stitch.

ROW 21: P1, k1, p1, k1, p1, join in yarn D (blue), k1D, [k2, k1D] rep 41 times more, p1, k1, p1, k1, p1. Cut yarn D (blue) 4 in. (10 cm) from the last stitch.

ROW 22: P1, k1, p1, k1, p1, join in yarn C (yellow), [p1, p2C] rep 41 times more, p2, k1, p1, k1, p1.

ROW 23: P1, k1, p1, k1, p1, k1, [k2C, k1] rep 41 times more, p1, k1, p1, k1, p1. Cut yarn C (yellow) 4 in. (10 cm) from the last stitch.

ROW 24: P1, k1, p1, k1, p1, join in yarn B (dark green), yarn, [p1B, p2] rep 41 times more, p1B, p1, k1, p1, k1, p1. Cut yarn B (dark green) 4 in. (10 cm) from the last stitch.

ROW 25 (BUTTONHOLE ROW): P1, k1, yo twice, k2tog, p1, knit to last 5 sts, p1, k1, p1, k1, p1.

ROW 26 (COMPLETE BUTTONHOLE ROW): P1, k1, p1, k1, purl to last 4 sts, drop the first loop of the double yo, purl yo loop, k1, p1.

The numbers in the squares refer to instructions in the Workshop sections.

119

ROW 27: P1, k1, p1, k1, p1, knit to last 5 sts, p1, k1, p1, k1, p1.

ROW 28: P1, k1, p1, k1, purl to last 4 sts, k1, p1, k1, p1. Rep rows 27–28 until 10 rows have been completed from the last buttonhole row.

ROW 37 (BUTTONHOLE ROW): P1, k1, yo twice, k2tog, p1, knit to last 5 sts, p1, k1, p1, k1, p1.

ROW 38 (COMPLETE BUTTONHOLE ROW): P1, k1, p1, k1, purl to last 4 sts, drop the first loop of the double yo, purl yo loop, k1, p1.

Rep rows 27–28 four times more until a total of 46 rows have been completed.

Check the depth from the cast-on edge. This will be the measurement from the hem to the underarm and should be about 6 in. (15 cm). The jacket can be lengthened at this point, but remember to create a buttonhole every 10 rows on the right edge, and if only a few rows are added, the position of the top buttonhole will change.

Divide for the front and back

ROW 47: P1, k1, p1, k1, p1, k29, place these 34 sts onto a stitch holder. Bind (cast) off 6 sts, k56 sts, place these 57 sts onto a stitch holder. Bind (cast) off 6 sts, k28, p1, k1, p1, k1, p1. The 34 sts on the needle form the left front.

Left front

The edge without the seed (moss) stitch becomes the armhole edge.

Shape armhole

ROW 48: P1, k1, p1, k1, purl to last 3 sts, **purl one, pass the next stitch over (ppno)** 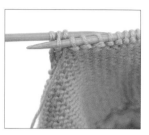**, then pass stitch back to right-hand needle, p1.

ROW 49: K1, **slip one, knit one, pass the slipped stitch over (skpo)** , knit to last 5 sts, p1, k1, p1, k1, p1.

Rep rows 48–49 once more. *(30 sts)*

ROW 52: P1, k1, p1, k1, purl to end of row.

ROW 53: Knit to last 5 sts, p1, k1, p1, k1, p1.

The numbers in the squares refer to instructions in the Workshop sections.

Rep rows 52–53 until a total of 69 rows have been worked.

Shape neck

ROW 70: Bind (cast) off 8 sts keeping the seed (moss) stitch patt correct. Purl to end of row.

(22 sts)

ROW 71: Knit to last 2 sts, k1, slip the last stitch back onto the left-hand needle,

pass second stitch over, then slip stitch onto right-hand needle.

(21 sts)

ROW 72: Sl1, p1, pass the slip stitch over, purl to end of the row.

(20 sts)

Rep rows 71–72 until 14 sts remain on the needle and 6 more rows have been worked.

ROW 79: Knit.

ROW 80: Purl. Bind (cast) off.

Back

This is the section of stitches next to the left front.

With the WS facing, pass the 57 stitches off the stitch holder so that the last stitch onto the needle is also the last one knitted.

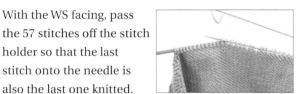

ROW 48: P1, **purl two stitches together (p2tog)** [20], purl to last 3 sts,

ppno, p1.

(55 sts)

ROW 49: K1, skpo, knit to last 3 sts,

knit two stitches together (k2tog) [11], k1.

(53 sts)

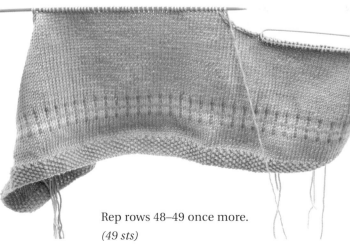

Rep rows 48–49 once more.

(49 sts)

ROW 52: Purl.

ROW 53: Knit.

Rep rows 52–53 until a total of 78 rows have been completed.

Shape neck

ROW 79: K15, bind (cast) off 19 sts, k14.

(15 sts + 15 sts)

ROW 80: Purl to the last 2 sts, ppno.

ROW 81: Bind (cast) off 14 sts.

Cut the yarn 4 in. (10 cm) from the last stitch and rejoin to p2tog, purl the rem 13 sts on the needle on the other side of the back neckline.

Bind (cast) off 14 sts.

Right front

This is the last section of stitches.

With the WS facing, pass the stitches off the stitch holder so that the last stitch onto the needle is also the last one knitted.

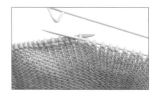

Shape armhole

ROW 48: P1, p2tog, purl to last 4 sts, k1, p1, k1, p1.

(33 sts)

ROW 49 (BUTTONHOLE ROW): P1, k1, yo twice, k2tog, p1, knit to last 3 sts, k2tog, k1.

(32 sts)

ROW 50 (COMPLETE BUTTONHOLE ROW): P1, p2tog, purl to last 4 sts, drop the first loop of the double yo, purl yo loop, k1, p1.

ROW 51: P1, k1, p1, k1, p1, knit to last 3 sts, k2tog, k1.

(30 sts)

ROW 52: Purl to last 4 sts, k1, p1, k1, p1.

ROW 53: P1, k1, p1, k1, p1, knit to end of row.

Rep rows 52–53 until a total of 60 rows have been worked.

ROW 61 (BUTTONHOLE ROW): P1, k1, yo twice, k2tog, p1, knit to end of row.

ROW 62 (COMPLETE BUTTONHOLE ROW): Purl to last 4 sts, drop the first loop of the double yo, purl yo loop, k1, p1.

Work six more rows in patt set.

Shape neck

ROW 69: Bind (cast) off 8 sts keeping the seed (moss) stitch patt correct. Knit to end of row. *(22 sts)*

ROW 70: Purl to last 2 sts, p1, slip last stitch back onto the left-hand needle,

pass the second stitch over. *(21 sts)*

ROW 71: Skpo, knit to end of row. *(20 sts)*

Rep rows 70–71 until only 14 sts remain on the needle and 6 more rows have been completed.

ROW 78: Purl.
ROW 79: Knit.
ROW 80: Purl.
Bind (cast) off.

Sleeve

Make a slip knot 24 in. (60 cm) from the end of the yarn and, using the thumb cast-on method and US 4 (3.5mm) needles, cast on 37 sts.

ROW 1: [K1, p1] to last st, k1.
ROW 2: [P1, k1] to last st, p1.

Rows 1–2 form a rib patt. Rep these rows until 6 rows have been worked.

Change to US 6 (4mm) needles. The rest of the sleeve is worked in St st with increases and decreases to shape the sleeve as required.

ROW 7: K2, **make one (m1) 26**,

knit to last 2 sts, m1, k2. *(39 sts)*

ROW 8: Purl.
ROW 9: Knit.
ROW 10: Purl.
ROW 11: K2, m1, knit to last 2 sts, m1, k2. *(41 sts)*
ROW 12–14: Work in St st.
ROW 15: K2, m1, knit to last 2 sts, m1, k2. *(43 sts)*
ROW 16–18: Work in St st.
ROW 19: K2, m1, knit to last 2 sts, m1, k2. *(45 sts)*
ROW 20–22: Work in St st.
ROW 23: K2, m1, knit to last 2 sts, m1, k2. *(47 sts)*

ROW 24–26: Work in St st.

ROW 27: K2, m1, knit to last 2 sts, m1, k2.
(49 sts)

ROW 28–30: Work in St st.

ROW 31: K2, m1, knit to last 2 sts, m1, k2.
(51 sts)

ROW 32–34: Work in St st.

ROW 35: K2, m1, knit to last 2 sts, m1, k2.
(53 sts)

ROW 36–38: Work in St st.

ROW 39: K2, m1, knit to last 2 sts, m1, k2.
(55 sts)

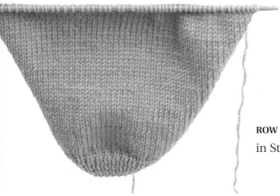

ROW 40–42: Work in St st patt set.

At this point the sleeve can be lengthened. The sleeve should measure 6 in. (15 cm) from the cast-on edge. If necessary work more rows in St st without shaping, ending with a WS row.

Now shape the sleeve cap to fit the armhole.

ROW 43: K2, skpo,

knit to last 4 sts, k2tog, k2.
(53 sts)

ROW 44: P2, p2tog, purl to last 4 sts, ppno, p2.
(51 sts)

ROW 45: Knit.

There are two decrease rows in every three rows worked.

ROW 46: P2, p2tog, purl to last 4 sts, ppno, p2.

ROW 47: K2, k2tog, knit to last 4 sts, skpo, p2.
(47 sts)

ROW 48: Purl.

ROW 49: K2, k2tog, knit to last 4 sts, skpo, p2.

ROW 50: P2, p2tog, purl to last 4 sts, ppno, p2.
(43 sts)

ROW 51: Knit.

ROW 52: P2, p2tog, purl to last 4 sts, ppno, p2.

ROW 53: K2, k2tog, knit to last 4 sts, skpo, p2.
(39 sts)

ROW 54: Purl.

ROW 55: K2, k2tog, knit to last 4 sts, skpo, p2.

ROW 56: P2, p2tog, purl to last 4 sts, ppno, p2.
(35 sts)

ROW 57: Knit.

ROW 58: P2, p2tog, purl to last 4 sts, ppno, p2.

ROW 59: K2, k2tog, knit to last 4 sts, skpo, p2.
(31 sts)

ROW 60: Purl.

ROW 61: K2, k2tog, knit to last 4 sts, skpo, p2.

ROW 62: P2, p2tog, purl to last 4 sts, ppno, p2.
(27 sts)

ROW 63: Knit.

ROW 64: P2, p2tog, purl to last 4 sts, ppno, p2.

ROW 65: K2, k2tog, knit to last 4 sts, skpo, p2.
(23 sts)

ROW 66: Purl.

Bind (cast) off.

To set the stitches of the color knitting in place, steam and press the reverse side of the color knitting firmly with a damp cloth. Take care not to flatten the seed (moss) stitch or to distress the yarn.

Block and press 🔢 the sleeve and body pieces carefully, making sure that the edges are straight and the measurements match the knitted measurements given at the beginning of the patt. Take particular care with the edges and wait until the pieces are completely dry before sewing them together.

Finishing

Lay the body out on a flat surface. Look carefully at the color knitting.

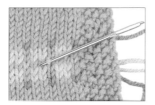
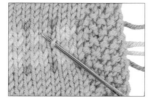

Any baggy or tight stitches can be eased by inserting a needle under one side of the stitch loop and then the other side.

Work along the rows systematically, ending at the beginning or end of a length of yarn that can be eased gently before securing.
If the background color needs some stitches adjusted, take up the slack in the strands of yarn on the wrong side or in other stitches on the row.

Weave in Fair Isle ends by picking up one upper ridge loop and then working under and over the same color strands in the knitting.

Using **mattress stitch** 🔢, sew the shoulder seams together and sew the sleeve seam.
Fold the sleeve in half with the seam forming one edge to find the center of the shoulder.

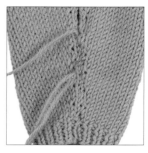

Use small pins to secure the sleeve to the body piece, aligning the sleeve seam with the center of the lower armhole and the top of the shoulder with the shoulder seam.

Use mattress stitch to sew the sleeve to the body piece. Start at the sleeve seam, leaving a loose tail of yarn.

Weave in ends 🔢 into the seams.
Sew the buttons securely to the seed (moss) stitch edge to align with the buttonholes.

The numbers in the squares refer to instructions in the Workshop sections.

Correcting mistakes

We all do it: even the most experienced knitter finds that from time to time they have dropped a stitch or forgotten part of the pattern repeat. The trick is to keep an eye on the work as it progresses. Check the stitch counts as you go and take the time to admire your knitting. However heartbreaking it may seem, the easiest and most effective way to correct mistakes is to unravel the knitting to a point beyond the error and re-knit, so try to spot any errors early.

Picking up stitches

The dropped stitch is one of the most common mishaps, but if spotted before it is missed on subsequent rows it is very easy to remedy.

On a knit row

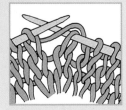

1 Knit to the point of the dropped stitch. With the stitch strand at the back, pick up the stitch with the right-hand needle from front to back.

2 Pass the stitch over the strand by inserting the left-hand needle through the back of the stitch and lifting it off the right-hand needle.

3 The strand has now created a stitch facing the wrong way on the right-hand needle. Slip the stitch onto the left-hand needle by inserting the needle from front to back. Continue knitting the row.

On a purl row

1 Purl to the point of the dropped stitch. With the stitch strand at the front, pick up the stitch with the right-hand needle from back to front.

2 Pass the stitch over the strand by inserting the left-hand needle through the front of the stitch and lifting it off the right-hand needle over the stitch strand. Slip the stitch onto the left-hand needle. Continue purling the row.

Prevention is better than cure

- **Sometimes stitches stand proud of the work, but the stitch count is correct.** Check whether a stitch has been split or not knitted cleanly from the left-hand needle. Unravel the work but note that the yarn may be susceptible to the problem.
- **The texture of stitches changes within a row.** This may have been caused by stopping mid-row. Try and finish a row before putting your knitting aside and don't knit when you are tired or stressed.

Unravelling

Sometimes several rows have gone by before an error is noticed. The only thing to do is to slide the stitches off the needle and gently pull the yarn, easing out the stitches and continuing one row beyond the error. It is quicker and easier to knit a couple of extra rows than to try to correct an error at its point of conception and disguise any damaged yarn. Put the stitches back onto the needle, starting with those farthest from the working yarn. If the stitches are difficult to pick up, try the technique below, which will also take the work back one more row.

On a knit row

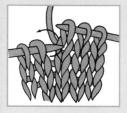

With the yarn at the back, pick up the stitch by inserting the left-hand needle from front to back into the stitch below the free loop. Drop the stitch above off the needle and pull the working yarn, withdrawing the stitch loop.

On a purl row

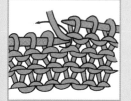

With the yarn in front, pick up the stitch by inserting the left-hand needle from front to back and continue as for a knit row.

Remember

A little time spent in reknitting is nothing compared to the potential years of looking at an otherwise perfect knitted project and saying "if only". Ask yourself, does it show? If it does, don't ignore it; deal with it.

Yarn information

Yarns come and go, and there is always the ball of yarn you fall in love with at first sight. This information will help you to substitute if yarns in this book are not available, and to decide whether your must-have yarn will work for a given project. Check the pattern, look at the ball bands, and compare with the information below before making your choice. Remember that the people who work in the store should be both knowledgeable and eager to help.

Rowan Kidsilk Haze
Very lightweight
mohair yarn
70% super kid mohair/
30% silk
Approximately 230 yds
(210 m) per 1 oz (25 g) ball

Rowan Cotton Glace
Lightweight cotton yarn
100% cotton
Approximately 125 yds
(115 m) per 1¾oz (50 g) ball

**Rowan Handknit
DK Cotton**
Medium weight cotton yarn
100% cotton
Approximately 92 yds
(85 m) per 1¾oz (50 g) ball

Rowan Denim
Medium weight cotton yarn
100% cotton
Approximately 101 yds
(93 m) per 1¾oz (50 g) ball

Rowan Wool Cotton
Double-knitting-weight wool
and cotton
50% merino wool/
50% cotton
Approximately 123 yds
(113m) per 1¾oz (50 g) ball

Rowan All Seasons Cotton
Aran-weight cotton and
microfiber yarn
60% cotton/
40% microfiber
Approximately 98 yds (90 m)
per 1¾oz (50 g) ball

**Rowan Yorkshire
Tweed Aran**
Aran-weight wool yarn
100% pure new wool
Approximately 175 yds
(160 m) per 3½oz
(100 g) hank

Rowan Yorkshire Tweed Chunky
Bulky-weight wool yarn
100% pure new wool
Approximately 109 yd
(100 m) per 3½ oz
(100 g) hank

Rowan Polar
Chunky-weight mix yarn
60% pure new wool,
30% alpaca, 10% acrylic
Approximately 109 yd
(100 m) per 3½ oz
(100 g) hank

Jaeger Matchmaker Merino DK
Medium weight wool yarn
100% merino wool
Approximately 130 yd
(120 m) per 1¾ oz (50 g) ball

Jaeger Shetland
Aran-weight mix yarn
80% wool, 20% alpaca
Approximately 153 yd
(107 m) per 3½ oz
(100 g) hank

Suppliers

Suppliers of Rowan Yarns and Jaeger Handknits

USA
Westminster Fibers Inc.
5 Northern Boulevard
Amherst
New Hampshire 03031
Tel: 603 886 5041/5043

Canada
Diamond Yarn
9697 St Laurent
Montreal
Quebec H3L 2N1
Tel: 514 388 6188

Diamond Yarn (Toronto)
155 Martin Ross
Unit 3
Toronto
Ontario M3J 2L9
Tel: 416 736 6111

Australia
Rowan at Sunspun
185 Canterbury Road
Canterbury
Victoria 3126
Tel: 03 9830 1609

UK
Rowan Yarns and Jaeger
Handknits
Green Lane Mill
Holmfirth
West Yorkshire
HD9 2DX
Tel: 01484 681881
www.knitrowan.com

Author acknowledgments

We would like to take this opportunity to thank in particular the following people for their kindness, tolerance and patience during the writing and designing of this book. We would be nowhere without the beautiful photographs of Mathew Dickens and modelling of Kelly Dickens, the pattern checking of Marilyn Wilson, and without Marie Clayton and Nicola Hodgson at Collins & Brown.
We would also like to thank Kate Buller of Rowan Yarns for her faith and support of the book and Ann Hinchcliffe for fufilling yarn requests so cheerfully and efficiently.
Thanks also to Mary Green and Tina Cook at Martingale & Company for their constructive input.

Lastly, Elvis and Olive Oil, for their love and affection.